Ace the
TOEFL Primary

Step 2 (Reading & Listening)

Contents

Introduction to the toefl primary®

■ About toefl primary®

toefl primary®는 미국 ETS(Educational Testing Service)에서 개발한 영어학습 입문 단계의 글로벌 영어 인증 시험입니다. 영어를 모국어로 사용하지 않는 나라의 어린 학습자들을 대상으로 전반적인 영어 능력을 측정합니다.

toefl primary®는 PBT(Paper Based Tests) 방식의 toefl primary® Reading and Listening Test – Step 1 & Step 2와 iBT(internet Based Tests) 방식의 toefl primary® Speaking & Writing Test가 있습니다.

■ Test Options

- **toefl primary® Reading and Listening Test – Step 1**
  - 영어를 시작하는 초기 단계의 학습자 대상
  - 익숙한 환경(학교, 집, 운동장 등)에서 발생하는 일상생활과 밀접한 주제
  - 친숙한 인물 또는 사물과 관련된 기초 어휘와 표현
  - 일상생활에 필요한 간단한 지시문 및 학습 관련 짧은 지문 이해

- **toefl primary® Reading and Listening Test – Step 2**
  - 영어 의사소통 능력이 발달되고 있는 중급 단계의 학습자 대상
  - 일상생활의 범위를 넘어선 주제와 관련된 짧은 스토리와 대화 내용 이해
  - 기본적인 표현, 요구사항, 지시사항
  - 교과 기반의 지문 이해

- **toefl primary® Speaking Test**
  - 일상생활과 관련된 상황에서 필요한 의사소통을 하기 위한 말하기 능력 평가
  - 기본적인 감정과 의견 표현
  - 간단한 요청 또는 지시사항 표현
  - 사람, 사물, 동물, 장소, 활동 묘사
  - 간단한 사건을 시간 순서대로 설명

- **toefl primary® Writing Test**
  - 일상생활과 관련된 친숙한 주제에 대해 글로 소통하는 쓰기 능력 평가
  - 사람, 물건, 동물, 상황, 장소 및 활동에 대한 내용 이해
  - 간단한 상황을 순서대로 쓰기
  - 짧고 일관된 스토리 작성하기

■ Test Structure

toefl primary₀ Reading and Listening Test – Step 1

영역	문항 수	샘플 문항 수	총 문항 수	시험 시간	점수	등급
Reading	36	3	39	30분	100~109	1-4 등급
Listening	36	5	41	30분	100~109	(☆로 표시)
Total	72	8	80	60분	200~218	

toefl primary₀ Reading and Listening Test – Step 2

영역	문항 수	샘플 문항 수	총 문항 수	시험 시간	점수	등급
Reading	36	1	37	30분	100~115	1-5 등급
Listening	36	3	39	35분	100~115	(🏅로 표시)
Total	72	4	76	65분	200~230	

toefl primary₀ Speaking Test

영역	문항 수	시험 시간	점수	등급
Speaking	7~10	20분	1~27	1-5 등급 (🏅로 표시)

toefl primary₀ Writing Test

영역	문항 수	시험 시간	점수	등급
Writing	19	30분	1~17	1-4 등급 (🏅로 표시)

※ toefl primary₀ 공식 웹사이트: http://www.toeflyss.or.kr

Ace the TOEFL Primary Step 2 – Reading

Part 1

2~3개의 문장으로 이루어진 짧은 설명과 세 개의 보기가 주어집니다. 설명에 해당하는 답을 고릅니다.

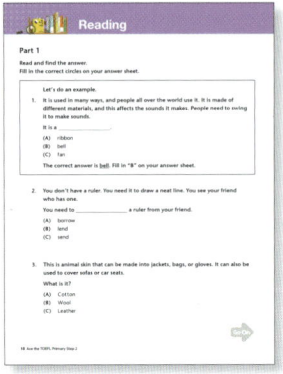

Part 2

초대장, 일정, 광고 등의 안내문(혹은 포스터) 및 이메일(혹은 편지), 지시문, 이야기, 교과 관련 내용 등을 읽고 2~4개의 관련 질문에 맞는 답을 고릅니다.

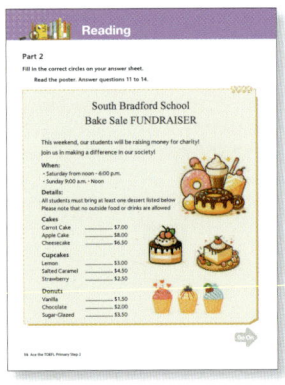
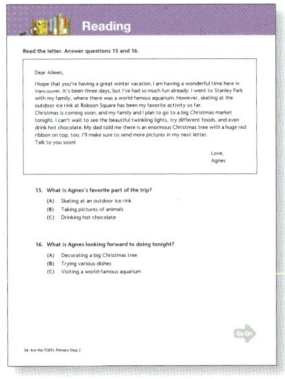
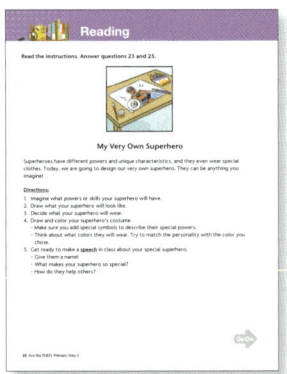
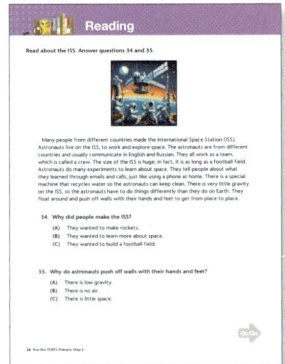

Ace the TOEFL Primary Step 2 – Listening

Part 1

세 개의 그림 보기가 주어지며, 들리는 지시사항을 가장 잘 따르거나 표현한 답을 고릅니다.

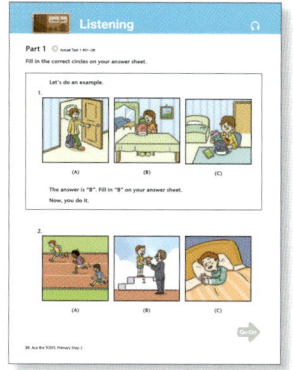

Part 2

두 사람의 대화를 들은 후, 대화에서 언급된 내용에 대한 질문에 답합니다.

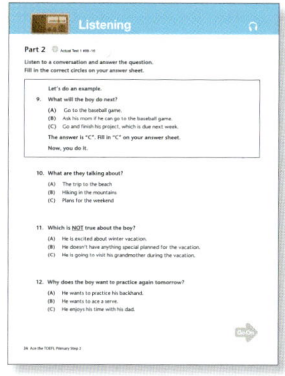

Part 3

전화 메시지를 들은 후, 전화를 건 목적이나 메시지에서 언급된 세부사항에 대한 질문에 맞는 답을 고릅니다.

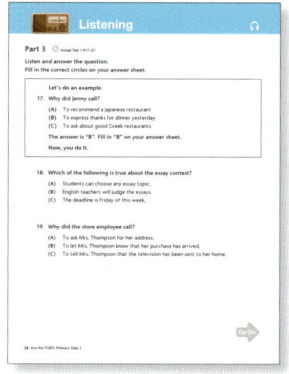

Part 4

이야기나 교과 관련 지문을 듣고 글의 요지 또는 세부사항 관련 3~4개의 질문에 맞는 답을 고릅니다.

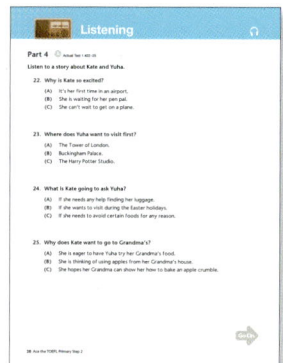

Actual Test 01

Reading

Part 1

Read and find the answer.

Fill in the correct circles on your answer sheet.

Let's do an example.

1. It is used in many ways, and people all over the world use it. It is made of different materials, and this affects the sounds it makes. People need to swing it to make sounds.

    It is a _____.

    (A) ribbon
    (B) bell
    (C) fan

    The correct answer is <u>bell</u>. Fill in "B" on your answer sheet.

---

2. You don't have a ruler. You need it to draw a neat line. You see your friend who has one.

    You need to _____ a ruler from your friend.

    (A) borrow
    (B) lend
    (C) send

3. This is animal skin that can be made into jackets, bags, or gloves. It can also be used to cover sofas or car seats.

    What is it?

    (A) Cotton
    (B) Wool
    (C) Leather

4. You are on stage. You receive a trophy and a certificate for your hard work at school. People are clapping for you.

    You feel _____.

    (A) proud
    (B) confused
    (C) anxious

5. You put in a lot of effort and time. You practice repeatedly to get better. You try your best to improve.

    Your skills will _____.

    (A) be declined
    (B) be enhanced
    (C) be decreased

6. These have ten numbers, 0-9. I can't play games or call my friends on them, but I can add, subtract, multiply and divide with them. They help me study.

    What are they?

    (A) Cameras
    (B) Calculators
    (C) Copy machines

7. People are sitting around a big table. They are looking at a presentation. They look like they are working.

    The people are _____.

    (A) communicating
    (B) cooking
    (C) collecting

8. You have recently joined a swimming club. You are learning how to hold your breath underwater, practicing kicks, and learning arm motions for simple strokes.

   You are _____ and improving every day.

   (A) getting cold feet

   (B) learning the ropes

   (C) biting your tongue

9. Your brother is having a birthday party. You decide to help him write the invitations. You have finished the invitations and want to send them.

   You put them in _____ .

   (A) images

   (B) arrows

   (C) envelopes

10. A lot of people usually study here. Some of these places are small and some are really large. There are desks and chairs and books here.

    What place is it?

    (A) A school

    (B) An office building

    (C) A hospital

Reading

Go On

Part 2

Fill in the correct circles on your answer sheet.

Read the poster. Answer questions 11 to 14.

South Bradford School
Bake Sale FUNDRAISER

This weekend, our students will be raising money for charity!

Join us in making a difference in our society!

When:
- Saturday from noon - 6:00 p.m.
- Sunday 9:00 a.m. - Noon

Details:
All students must bring at least one dessert listed below
Please note that no outside food or drinks are allowed

Cakes

Carrot Cake	....	$7.00
Apple Cake	....	$8.00
Cheesecake	....	$6.50

Cupcakes

Lemon	....	$3.00
Salted Caramel	....	$4.50
Strawberry	....	$2.50

Donuts

Vanilla	....	$1.50
Chocolate	....	$2.00
Sugar-Glazed	....	$3.50

11. **What should the students bring to the fundraiser?**

   (A)   Fried chicken

   (B)   Lemonade

   (C)   Cheesecake

12. **When will the bake sale end on Sunday?**

   (A)   6:00 p.m.

   (B)   4:00 p.m.

   (C)   12:00 p.m.

13. **What is the most expensive cake?**

   (A)   Cheesecake

   (B)   Carrot cake

   (C)   Apple cake

14. **Why is the school doing a bake sale?**

   (A)   To teach students how to bake

   (B)   To make a donation

   (C)   To win in the society bake sale

Reading

Read the letter. Answer questions 15 and 16.

Dear Aileen,

I hope that you're having a great winter vacation. I am having a wonderful time here in Vancouver. It's been three days, but I've had so much fun already. I went to Stanley Park with my family, where there was a world-famous aquarium. However, skating at the outdoor ice rink at Robson Square has been my favorite activity so far.

Christmas is coming soon, and my family and I plan to go to a big Christmas market tonight. I can't wait to see the beautiful twinkling lights, try different foods, and even drink hot chocolate. My dad told me there is an enormous Christmas tree with a huge red ribbon on top, too. I'll make sure to send more pictures in my next letter.

Talk to you soon!

Love,
Agnes

---

15. **What is Agnes's favorite part of the trip?**

   (A)   Skating at an outdoor ice rink

   (B)   Taking pictures of animals

   (C)   Drinking hot chocolate

16. **What is Agnes looking forward to doing tonight?**

   (A)   Decorating a big Christmas tree

   (B)   Trying various dishes

   (C)   Visiting a world-famous aquarium

Reading

Test 1

Read the e-mail. Answer questions 17 and 18.

To: Mr. Spencer
From: Emma
Subject: Graduation

Dear Mr. Spencer,

I can't believe that I am graduating tomorrow! I have learned so much here at Louisville School, and I just wanted to thank you for being a fantastic teacher. You taught me the importance of hard work, which has helped me in all my classes. I appreciated how you tried very hard to make sure that all students felt respected. You taught me and many other students to try their best with your patience and humor. Thank you again for encouraging me every step of the way.

With Respect,
Emma

17. Why did Emma write to Mr. Spencer?

(A) To thank him for the graduation party

(B) To thank him for being a great teacher

(C) To thank him for helping her teach students

18. What did Emma NOT learn from Mr. Spencer?

(A) Hard work

(B) Trying her best

(C) Humor

Go On

Reading

Read the e-mail. Answer questions 19 and 20.

To: Sean
From: Ian
Subject: Mom and Dad's Anniversary

I hope you're having a great week, Sean. I just wanted to let you know the details of our parents' anniversary this weekend. I reserved their favorite Italian restaurant for 7:00 p.m. and asked them to prepare mom's favorite lemon cake. All we have to do now is to pick up Uncle Leo and Aunt Julie from the train station on Saturday.
Since I have soccer practice late in the afternoon that day, could you pick up Uncle Leo and Aunt Julie from the train station? They will arrive around 5:00 p.m., and it would be great if you come straight to the restaurant with them.

Get back to me soon!

From,
Ian

19. **What is Ian asking Sean to do?**

   (A)   Make a reservation at an Italian restaurant

   (B)   Buy a lemon cake

   (C)   Pick Uncle Leo and Aunt Julie up from the train station

20. **At what time did Ian make a reservation at the restaurant?**

   (A)   5:00 p.m.

   (B)   6:00 p.m.

   (C)   7:00 p.m.

Read the letter. Answer questions 21 and 22.

Dear Students,

I am writing this letter to inform you that I will be taking a year off from teaching because I am going to travel to China for a year. I will miss each and every one of you. All of you are very talented and intelligent students. I have had a lot of fun teaching all of you this year. I have learned a lot from you all, and I hope you have learned something from me as well. If you need anything from me or would like to contact me, feel free to e-mail me, and I will get back to you as soon as I can.

Sincerely,
Ms. Richardson

---

21. How long will Ms. Richardson be traveling?

(A)   For a month

(B)   For one year

(C)   For one semester

22. Which of the following is <u>NOT</u> true about Ms. Richardson?

(A)   Students can contact her by phone.

(B)   She has learned a lot from her students.

(C)   She will miss all of her students.

Go On

Read the instructions. Answer questions 23 and 25.

My Very Own Superhero

Superheroes have different powers and unique characteristics, and they even wear special clothes. Today, we are going to design our very own superhero. They can be anything you imagine!

Directions:

1. Imagine what powers or skills your superhero will have.
2. Draw what your superhero will look like.
3. Decide what your superhero will wear.
4. Draw and color your superhero's costume.
   - Make sure you add special symbols to describe their special powers.
   - Think about what colors they will wear. Try to match the personality with the color you chose.
5. Get ready to make a **speech** in class about your special superhero.
   - Give them a name!
   - What makes your superhero so special?
   - How do they help others?

23. Why should you add symbols to your superhero costume?

(A)   To describe how tall they are

(B)   To describe the special powers they have

(C)   To describe how fast they are

24. Why should you think about the colors of your superhero costume?

(A)   To show how attractive they are

(B)   To help other superheroes

(C)   To show what kind of personality they have

25. In Step 5, what does <u>speech</u> mean?

(A)   Listen

(B)   Talk

(C)   Look

Go On

Read a story about Jenny's family. Answer questions 26 and 29.

Jenny's family is in their car, on their way to pick up Mia, a small Bichon Frise. They are talking about the responsibilities of having a dog as a new family member.

"Jenny, I know that you are very excited about bringing Mia home with us, but we must talk about the responsibilities we all have," Jenny's mother said.

"Of course, Mom! I have been watching videos and reading books about caring for dogs. There was so much useful information that I want to continue learning this way," replied Jenny.

"I'm proud that you've been putting your efforts in. Can you tell us what you learned?" Jenny's dad asked.

"Well, the first is that Mia must eat at least twice daily. Also, she will need fresh water all the time, since dogs drink a lot of water," replied Jenny.

"I'm impressed! Dogs do need to drink a lot, just like humans. They need to be hydrated, just like us," said her mom.

With excitement, Jenny responded, "Mia will drink more than other dogs because I will take her on long daily walks! On weekdays, I'll walk her straight after school and sometimes take her to the park to meet other dogs and play with them."

"That sounds like a good idea. On the weekends, we can take Mia to the beach or hiking with us," said her dad.

"That sounds so exciting! I hope that Mia can swim well like me one day! I wonder how Mia will feel when she sees the beautiful scenery when we go hiking together," Jenny said joyfully.

As they arrived at the parking lot, Jenny made a promise to herself. She promised that she would do her best to take good care of Mia so that her dog would have a wonderful life with her family.

26. **What is the story about?**

    (A)   A trip to the mountains

    (B)   A video about dogs

    (C)   A new family member

27. **How will Jenny take care of Mia?**

    (A)   By making food for her

    (B)   By taking Mia on long walks

    (C)   By taking her abroad

28. **Where will Jenny take Mia on weekdays?**

    (A)   To the park

    (B)   To the beach

    (C)   To the mountains

29. **Why is Jenny's mother impressed?**

    (A)   Jenny drinks a lot of water.

    (B)   Jenny knew that dogs need to drink a lot of water.

    (C)   Jenny knew Mia wanted to drink a lot of water.

Test 1

Go On

Read a story about Tommy and his mom. Answer questions 30 and 33.

Tommy and his mom are at their local grocery store and going over their weekly grocery list. Tommy's mom notices that he is frowning over the listed items and decides to tell him about the importance of a balanced meal.

"Tommy, let's play a game. I am going to describe what items we need, and you're going to guess what they are!" said Tommy's mom.
Feeling much better, Tommy replied, "Sounds fun! What's the first question?"
"Well, we need this to grow strong bones and teeth. It is usually white, and people need to put this in their refrigerators to keep it cold and fresh," said his mom.
Tommy laughed, "I know the answer! Milk! You tell me to drink a cup every day."
"That's right! Then, on to the next question. It is small and comes in many colors and shapes. It is in salads, pasta, and even stews. Can you guess what it is?" asked his mom.
A picture of small black and white pebbles entered his mind. "Beans!" he cried out, "Beans contain a lot of protein, and protein helps produce energy and build strong muscles!"
"Excellent! Are you ready for the last question? I'll give you a hint: it's one of your favorite vegetables. It is round and small, has brown skin, and people usually peel off the skin before using it," said Tommy's mom.
"I know this one for sure! Potatoes, right? I love how you can use it to make all kinds of tasty meals. It also contains fiber, which helps people digest and even sleep better," he answered.

Having so much fun, Tommy realized how eating healthy can be enjoyable.

30. Where is this story taking place?

(A)   At a department store

(B)   At a storehouse

(C)   At a supermarket

31. What is the story about?

(A)   Getting ingredients for dinner

(B)   Why it is important to go grocery shopping

(C)   Learning how eating healthy can also be fun

32. Why does Tommy's mom tell Tommy to drink milk every day?

(A)   It is his favorite drink.

(B)   It can help him grow strong bones.

(C)   It is always in the refrigerator.

33. What was <u>NOT</u> the answer to a question in the game?

(A)   Beans

(B)   Potatoes

(C)   Sausages

Go On

Reading

Read about the ISS. Answer questions 34 and 35.

Many people from different countries made the International Space Station (ISS). Astronauts live on the ISS, to work and explore space. The astronauts are from different countries and usually communicate in English and Russian. They all work as a team, which is called a crew. The size of the ISS is huge; in fact, it is as long as a football field. Astronauts do many experiments to learn about space. They tell people about what they learned through emails and calls, just like using a phone at home. There is a special machine that recycles water so the astronauts can keep clean. There is very little gravity on the ISS, so the astronauts have to do things differently than they do on Earth. They float around and push off walls with their hands and feet to get from place to place.

34. **Why did people make the ISS?**

   (A)   They wanted to make rockets.

   (B)   They wanted to learn more about space.

   (C)   They wanted to build a football field.

35. **Why do astronauts push off walls with their hands and feet?**

   (A)   There is low gravity.

   (B)   There is no air.

   (C)   There is little space.

Reading

Go On

Read about hibernation and estivation. Answer questions 36 and 37.

Hibernation is when some animals spend the cold winter sleeping for a long time. They do this to survive because there is not much food and the weather is too cold. Before they hibernate, some animals eat a lot of food and can double their usual body weight to help them survive. Also, they need to find a place where they can sleep. Usually, animals go into warm and dark places like dens to keep themselves safe and warm. When animals go into hibernation, their body temperature drops considerably, and their breathing rate slows. Many hibernators go into a deep sleep from October to November and wake up during March or April. Estivation is the complete opposite. Estivation is when some animals sleep for a long time in the summer. They estivate to survive the extreme heat as it can be just as dangerous as surviving the cold winter. When they estivate, animals do not have to hunt, which can help them save energy and keep away from the hot sun.

36. **Why do animals eat a lot of food before entering hibernation?**

   (A)   They have spent all their energy sleeping.

   (B)   They need to store fat to stay alive.

   (C)   They share the food with the other animals.

37. **What is the difference between hibernation and estivation?**

   (A)   Sleeping during the day or sleeping at night

   (B)   Sleeping on land or sleeping in water

   (C)   Sleeping in cold weather or sleeping in hot weather

You finished the reading test.

Do not mark questions 38 and 39.

No test questions on this page

Part 1 Actual Test 1 #01~08

Fill in the correct circles on your answer sheet.

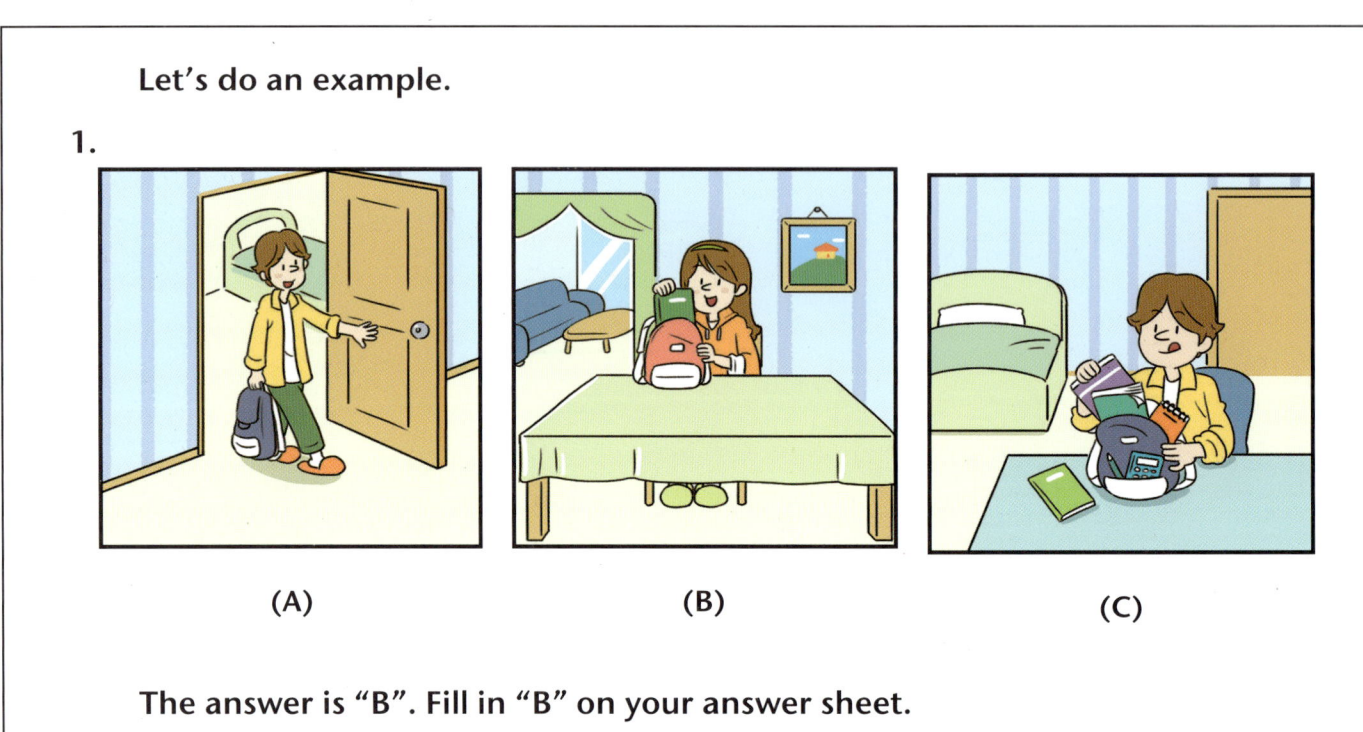

Let's do an example.

1.

(A) (B) (C)

The answer is "B". Fill in "B" on your answer sheet.

Now, you do it.

2.

(A) (B) (C)

3.

(A)

(B)

(C)

4.

(A)

(B)

(C)

5.

(A)

(B)

(C)

6.

(A)

(B)

(C)

7.

(A)

(B)

(C)

8.

(A)

(B)

(C)

Go On

Test 1

Listening

Listen to a conversation and answer the question.
Fill in the correct circle on your answer sheet.

Let's do an example.

9. **What will the boy do next?**

    (A) Go to the baseball game.

    (B) Ask his mom if he can go to the baseball game.

    (C) Go and finish his project, which is due next week.

    The answer is "C". Fill in "C" on your answer sheet.

    Now, you do it.

---

10. **What are they talking about?**

    (A) The trip to the beach

    (B) Hiking in the mountains

    (C) Plans for the weekend

11. **Which is <u>NOT</u> true about the boy?**

    (A) He is excited about winter vacation.

    (B) He doesn't have anything special planned for the vacation.

    (C) He is going to visit his grandmother during the vacation.

12. **Why does the boy want to practice again tomorrow?**

    (A) He wants to practice his backhand.

    (B) He wants to ace a serve.

    (C) He enjoys his time with his dad.

13. What does the girl want to do?

    (A)   She wants to meet Daisy in France.

    (B)   She wants to hear all about Daisy's trip to Spain.

    (C)   She wants to call Daisy to ask her about her trip.

14. What did the front desk ask the man?

    (A)   The number of people checking in.

    (B)   The man's personal information.

    (C)   The total number of rooms he wants to book.

15. Why is the boy feeling nervous?

    (A)   He has trouble memorizing his lines.

    (B)   He hasn't prepared for Mrs. Thatcher's class.

    (C)   He freezes up when he's on stage.

16. Why does the girl need her science project?

    (A)   To show it to her friends.

    (B)   She needs to turn it in to her teacher.

    (C)   She needs it for the science fair today.

Test 1

Go On

Part 3 Actual Test 1 #17~21

Listen and answer the question.

Fill in the correct circle on your answer sheet.

Let's do an example.

17. Why did Jenny call?

(A) To recommend a Japanese restaurant

(B) To express thanks for dinner yesterday

(C) To ask about good Greek restaurants

The answer is "B". Fill in "B" on your answer sheet.

Now, you do it.

---

18. Which of the following is true about the essay contest?

(A) Students can choose any essay topic.

(B) English teachers will judge the essays.

(C) The deadline is Friday of this week.

19. Why did the store employee call?

(A) To ask Mrs. Thompson for her address.

(B) To let Mrs. Thompson know that her purchase has arrived.

(C) To tell Mrs. Thompson that the television has been sent to her home.

20. **What will Daniel do tomorrow?**

    (A)   Add pictures to the family album.

    (B)   Do a presentation on family at school.

    (C)   Give back the family album.

21. **Why did Mr. Chancelor call Diane?**

    (A)   To make a plan for the fundraising sale.

    (B)   To thank her for bringing in the signed books.

    (C)   To ask if she can create a poster for the event.

Test 1

Part 4 Actual Test 1 #22~25

Listen to a story about Kate and Yuha.

22. Why is Kate so excited?

(A) It's her first time in an airport.

(B) She is waiting for her pen pal.

(C) She can't wait to get on a plane.

23. Where does Yuha want to visit the most?

(A) The Tower of London.

(B) Buckingham Palace.

(C) The Harry Potter Studio.

24. What is Kate going to ask Yuha?

(A) If she needs any help finding her luggage.

(B) If she wants to visit during the Easter holidays.

(C) If she needs to avoid certain foods for any reason.

25. Why does Kate want to go to Grandma's?

(A) She is eager to have Yuha try her Grandma's food.

(B) She is thinking of using apples from her Grandma's house.

(C) She hopes her Grandma can show her how to bake an apple crumble.

 Actual Test 1 #26~29

Listen to a story about Shelby.

26. What is the story about?

(A) How Shelby will overcome her fear.

(B) How Shelby will hang on to her fears.

(C) How Shelby is nervous about her speech competition.

27. Why did Shelby lose her confidence?

(A) Many people did a much better job than she did.

(B) There were too many people at the competition.

(C) Her mind blanked out when she was on the stage.

28. What did Shelby's mom and dad <u>NOT</u> say?

(A) That every mistake is a chance to improve.

(B) That all people were encouraging her at the speech.

(C) There's no harm done if something slips her mind.

29. How did Shelby gain her determination?

(A) She decided to gather her courage and go for it.

(B) She chose to buy some time and go for the next chance.

(C) She promised to put more effort into remembering her lines.

Listening

Actual Test 1 #30~33

Listen to a teacher talking in a history class.

30. Why do some countries have national flowers?

   (A) All countries had to have one in the past.

   (B) Flowers grow in every country in the world.

   (C) They represent a country's culture and history.

31. What does <u>NOT</u> describe the flowers mentioned in the passage?

   (A) The national flower of the U.S. is the rose.

   (B) The pink lotus can't grow well in muddy water.

   (C) People often give carnations at graduations.

32. Which flower was mentioned as a national flower?

   (A) The carnation

   (B) The pink lotus

   (C) The white lily

33. What is true about Italy?

   (A) Italy doesn't have a national flower.

   (B) White lilies grow well in muddy water in Italy.

   (C) Many people think the rose is the flower that stands for Italy.

 Actual Test 1 #34~36

Listen to a teacher talking in a science class.

34. What were pencils like a long time ago?

    (A)   Cheap and easy to use

    (B)   Costly and poisonous

    (C)   Harmless but expensive

35. How did people make the wood for the pencils hollow?

    (A)   They filled the wood with graphite.

    (B)   They added clay to the graphite.

    (C)   They filled the graphite with wood.

36. Why does the teacher talk about numbers and letters?

    (A)   To indicate the length of the pencils

    (B)   To point out how darkness is important in pencils

    (C)   To describe the levels of darkness in pencils

Listening

Listen to a teacher talking in an astronomy museum.

37. **How has the development of technology helped scientists?**

   (A) They can listen to the sounds of planets.

   (B) They can know about the entire universe.

   (C) They can understand much more about space.

38. **Which important job does the Sun <u>NOT</u> do?**

   (A) It spins the Earth.

   (B) It powers the water cycle.

   (C) It controls the weather patterns.

39. **Which planet takes the least time to orbit the Sun?**

   (A) Mercury

   (B) Earth

   (C) Neptune

You finished the listening test.

Do not mark questions 40 and 41.

No test questions on this page

Actual Test 02

Part 1

Read and find the answer.
Fill in the correct circles on your answer sheet.

Let's do an example.

1. People stand on this. It is a short and flat board, usually with four wheels. You can move forward by pushing one foot on the ground.

    It's a _____.

    (A) bicycle
    (B) skateboard
    (C) motorcycle

    The correct answer is <u>skateboard</u>. Fill in "B" on your answer sheet.

---

2. You are waiting in a very long line. There are many people in front of you. The line is getting shorter. You can now see the front gate.

    You will _____.

    (A) exit
    (B) exist
    (C) enter

3. You want to buy a big toy. You need more money to buy it. It costs more than other toys in the store.

    The toy is _____.

    (A) expensive
    (B) price
    (C) spend

4. She is walking through a store. She picks up pears, eggs and milk, puts them in her cart, and walks to the checkout.

   What is she doing?

   (A) Buying groceries

   (B) Selling fruit

   (C) Trading cards

5. Your family moved to a different city last year. You didn't want to move at first, but you made new friends and are enjoying your new school.

   Moving to a different city was _____.

   (A) a blessing in disguise

   (B) breaking the ice

   (C) a fish out of water

6. The rocket is about to be launched. People are counting down the numbers. They can see astronauts waving to the people.

   The astronauts are _____.

   (A) honest

   (B) brave

   (C) humble

7. The woman is caring for animals. She gives medicine to the sick animals. They get better after getting medical care.

   She is a _____.

   (A) veterinarian

   (B) mechanic

   (C) reporter

Go On

8. You need to put it on an envelope. It is payment in advance for delivery to another area or country. You can buy it in the post office.

What is it?

(A) A postcard

(B) An address

(C) A postage stamp

9. Your grandfather tells you that listening to others is important. This can build trust and help people understand each other.

Your grandfather has _____.

(A) delight

(B) actions

(C) wisdom

10. You are playing with your friends at a pool. There are many tubes in the swimming pool. You can see that they are on top of the water.

The tubes are _____.

(A) floating

(B) falling

(C) greeting

11. There are birds busily gathering twigs, leaves, and grass. They are making a little home in a tree.

It is a _____.

(A) den

(B) nest

(C) pond

Reading

Part 2

Fill in the correct circles on your answer sheet.

Read the poster. Answer questions 12 to 15.

Martins School Drama Club
A Week of Theater Magic!

This week, our students will be acting out famous plays and musicals for all students and parents.

Please come and support our talented students and enjoy their outstanding performances!

Monday	A Midsummer Night's Dream	5:00 p.m.	Auditorium
Tuesday	Alice in Wonderland	5:30 p.m.	Drama Studio
Wednesday	The Jungle Book	6:00 p.m.	Auditorium
Thursday	A Christmas Carol	6:30 p.m.	Gymnasium
Friday	Peter Pan	4:30 p.m.	Drama Studio

Ticket Cost

Drama Club Students: $3

Non-Drama Club Students: $5

Parents: $10

All money from ticket sales will be donated to charity

Be sure to arrive early, since all seats are first come, first served!

12. **What play is <u>NOT</u> included in the schedule?**

 (A)   Alice in Wonderland

 (B)   Hansel and Gretel

 (C)   A Christmas Carol

13. **Where will the students be performing on Thursday?**

 (A)   Drama Studio

 (B)   Auditorium

 (C)   Gymnasium

14. **Where will the ticket funds probably go?**

 (A)   To a swimming pool

 (B)   To the Drama Club

 (C)   To an environmental foundation

15. **What does the notice emphasize?**

 (A)   To participate in one of the plays

 (B)   To come as quickly as possible

 (C)   To help out in getting ready for a play

Go On

Reading

Read the e-mail. Answer questions 16 and 17.

To: Teacher Luke
From: Teacher Tiffany
Subject: School Fair

Hi Luke, this is Tiffany. I have some exciting news! Did you hear that the theme for this year's school fair is Harry Potter? I have a couple of interesting ideas that I think will help make the school fair more exciting. I was thinking of assigning students to different houses. It would be great if they could wear the Hogwarts uniforms while also having a wand. Also, how about playing songs from the movies all day long?
As you're the art teacher, I know you will be very busy decorating the whole school. So please let me know if there is anything that I can do to help.

Best,
Tiffany

16. **What ideas did Teacher Tiffany NOT give?**

    (A) Making a wand
    (B) Wearing the Hogwarts uniform
    (C) Listening to music

17. **Why did Teacher Tiffany write a letter?**

    (A) To ask if Teacher Luke is excited about this year's school fair
    (B) To ask if Teacher Luke can help her decorate the school
    (C) To ask if Teacher Luke needs help decorating the school

Reading

Read the e-mail. Answer questions 18 and 19.

To: Students
From: Ms. Vivian
Subject: Cooking class

I know you have all been wondering what we'll make in our cooking class next week. The three most popular menu items were spaghetti and meatballs, caramel apple cake, and broccoli soup. However, the most popular vote was for spaghetti and meatballs. As our cooking class is next Thursday, make sure that you do not forget to bring your ingredients.
Not only will we be having fun, but in our cooking class, we will also learn the importance of making healthier choices in our everyday meals. Eating nutritious meals is important for eating well and having a balanced meal.
Hope you have a good day.

From,
Ms. Vivian

18. **What will the students be making next Thursday?**

(A)   Spaghetti and meatballs

(B)   Caramel apple cake

(C)   Broccoli soup

19.   **What does Ms. Vivian want her students to learn?**

(A)   To be great chefs

(B)   To learn how to cook different menus

(C)   To learn the importance of a balanced meal

Read the instructions. Answer questions 20 to 22.

Getting Creative With Clay

Playing with clay and making fun objects is a great way for people to get creative. They can roll, cut, and shape clay however they want. This can allow them to transform a mold of clay into unique objects. Today, we will be making a cup of your design!

<u>Materials Needed:</u>

Clay (color of your choice)
A rolling pin
A plastic knife
A toothpick

<u>Directions:</u>

1. Play with your clay — Make it soft by squishing it.
2. Use your rolling pin, and make the clay flat and smooth.
3. Cut the clay into three shapes: a big rectangle, a small circle, and a long line.
4. Sides: roll the big rectangle into the shape of a cup and press the ends together.
5. Stick the small circle onto the bottom of your clay and gently press it to make it stick.
6. Handle: Take your line and bend it to make it a "c" shape.
7. Stick the end of the handle onto the side of your clay.
8. Use your fingers and toothpick to design it.
9. Cover your clay with baking paper.
   - It is ready to be put in the oven for baking. (Make sure that you ask your teacher for help!)

20. **What should you do after cutting the clay into different shapes?**

    (A)   Play with it to make it soft.

    (B)   Curl the rectangle into a cup shape.

    (C)   Use a toothpick to design your clay.

21. **Where do you have to stick the small circle?**

    (A)   At the bottom of your clay

    (B)   At the side of your clay

    (C)   At the center of your clay

22. **What should you do after covering the cup with baking paper?**

    (A)   Cool it

    (B)   Bake it

    (C)   Soften it

Go On

Read the instructions. Answer questions 23 to 25.

Get Creative With Toothpicks

Toothpicks are used in various ways. They can be used for cooking, building towers, cleaning, or creating different shapes. Many people get creative by making objects with them. Today, you will be learning how to make a hedgehog! It's very easy to make, so maybe you can even create a whole hedgehog family!

Materials Needed:

Clay (Light Brown)
Toothpicks (Around 20~30)
Colored paper (black for the eyes and nose, pink for the feet)
Scissors and glue

Directions:

- Make your clay soft by squishing it.
- To make a hedgehog body, shape the clay into an oval shape.
- Lightly pinch one side of the body to make a face.
- Cut out three black small circles for the eyes and nose.
- Then, cut four small pink ovals for the feet.
- Glue the eyes and nose on the hedgehog's face.
- Then, glue the feet on the bottom of the hedgehog's body.
- Take your toothpicks and stick them into the clay to make the spikes.
- Try to be careful with the toothpicks as they can be sharp at the ends.

23. Why do you need to cut colored paper?

(A)   To cover the body

(B)   To make the eyes and nose

(C)   To make the spikes

24. What do you have to do after cutting the colored paper?

(A)   Pinch one side of the hedgehog's body.

(B)   Stick the toothpicks inside the clay.

(C)   Glue the cut shapes onto the hedgehog's body.

25. Where should you stick the pink-colored oval shapes?

(A)   On the hedgehog's face

(B)   On the hedgehog's body

(C)   On the hedgehog's feet

Go On

Reading

Read a story about Violet and Daisy. Answer questions 26 to 29.

"Hey, Violet, I can't believe we're on the same team for the science project," Daisy exclaimed. "I'm so glad that we're finally on the same team! Let's make the best project our school has ever seen!" replied Violet.

The two girls have been learning about the solar system at school. They have learned the planets Mercury, Venus, Earth, Mars, Jupiter, Saturn, Uranus, and Neptune in great detail. Their project is to make a planet of their own. This planet must include at least one special feature of three different planets.

"How about we design our planet like Mercury? I think placing our planet closest to the Sun would be interesting, just like Mercury," said Daisy.
"That sounds like a great idea! And how about we make our planet the largest one, just like Jupiter?" suggested Violet.
"I agree! Let's make it twice as large as Jupiter! It will be so big that it will surprise all of our friends in class!" cried Daisy.
"That sounds like a plan. What should we do with the color? I was thinking about the colors... maybe yellow like Venus, red like Mars, or deep blue like Neptune?" said Violet.
"Hmm... I know your favorite color matches mine, so how about we color it blue?" asked Daisy.
"That sounds perfect! Now that we've decided on the features of our planet, how about we meet tomorrow after school to make it?" Violet suggested.
Thinking about what she had to do tomorrow, Daisy said, "I have to check with my mom first, so is it OK if I let you know by tonight?"
"No problem; just call me when you have an answer! We also have to go to the market to pick up the materials we need for our planet," Violet replied.
"Absolutely! I'll call you tonight!" Daisy said as she waved goodbye to Violet.

26. What must students do for their science project?

(A)　A speech on the solar system.

(B)　An individual project about a planet they studied.

(C)　Create their own planet.

27. What three planets will Violet and Daisy consider when making their planet?

(A)　Mercury, Venus, and Neptune

(B)　Mercury, Neptune, and Jupiter

(C)　Mercury, Jupiter, and Mars

28. What color will they probably paint their planet?

(A)　Yellow

(B)　Red

(C)　Blue

29. Why will Daisy call Violet later tonight?

(A)　To tell her whether or not she can meet tomorrow

(B)　To say whether she got all the materials from the market

(C)　To remind her to call the market tomorrow

Read a story about Aaron and his family. Answer questions 30 to 33.

It was a warm Saturday afternoon, and Aaron and his family had just arrived at the photo studio for their yearly family photo. All their family members had arrived and were all excited to have their photo taken.

"Mom, can I sit in the middle? I want to sit next to Grandpa. Daisy sat in the middle last time, so it's only fair if I sat in the middle this time!" cried Aaron.
"Sure you can! But Aaron, can you please tuck your shirt in before we take the photo?" asked Aaron's mom.
Quickly tucking his shirt in, Aaron raced to the middle of the photo booth, saying, "Daisy, I'm standing in the middle today!"
"Sure, I was going to stand next to Dad anyway; he promised to give me a piggyback ride," Daisy replied.
Getting the camera ready, the photographer asked, "Is everyone ready? We'll be taking the photo in ten minutes now! Please gather around."

Soon, all of Aaron's family gathered around, and they all put on their best smiles. Aaron loved taking family photos as he could always feel the connection and love between his family members.

"Taking family photos is one of my favorite things to do. I love how it reminds us of our memories with each other," Aaron's dad said.
"I think so too! But I also like seeing how much I grow and change over the years!" exclaimed Daisy.

30. How often does Aaron's family take family photos?

(A) Every week

(B) Every month

(C) Every year

31. Why did Aaron ask his mom if he could sit in the middle?

(A) He wanted to sit next to Daisy.

(B) He wanted to sit next to Dad.

(C) He wanted to sit next to Grandpa.

32. What does Aaron have to do before taking the family picture?

(A) He needs to tell grandpa that he will sit next to him.

(B) He needs to tuck in his shirt.

(C) He needs to tell the photographer that they are ready.

33. Why does Daisy like to take family photos?

(A) She likes seeing how she changes and grows.

(B) She likes wearing pretty clothes and make-up.

(C) She likes to take pictures.

Go On

Reading

Read about different types of animals. Answer questions 34 and 35.

    The animal kingdom is full of different animal species. Most are divided into different animal groups. Out of the various types, three types of animals are categorized based on what they eat. The first is the carnivores. These animals eat meat, meaning they eat other animals. However, they sometimes eat plants to manage their diets. Carnivores tend to have sharp teeth, which they use to catch prey. Wolves, lions, and tigers are typical examples of this type of animal. Animals that eat plants are called herbivores. They have flat teeth to grind and chew plants into small pieces. Examples include elephants, giraffes, and camels. Last, the all eaters, omnivores. Omnivores have both sharp and flat teeth for tearing and chewing food. Famous examples are bears, chimpanzees, and, of course, humans!

34. **Based on the passage, in what ways are the animals divided?**

    (A) Eating habits

    (B) Sleeping habits

    (C) Hunting habits

35. **What types of teeth were <u>NOT</u> mentioned in the passage?**

    (A) Wisdom teeth

    (B) Sharp teeth

    (C) Flat teeth

Read about Helen Keller. Answer questions 36 and 37.

Helen Keller is one of the world's most famous and celebrated heroes and activists. She was just like any other ordinary child, but when she was just 19 months old, she got very ill and lost her eyesight and her hearing. As she couldn't communicate with people, she had difficulty expressing her thoughts and feelings and often got frustrated. When she was six years old, she met her teacher, Anne Sullivan, and they had a lifelong friendship. Anne taught Helen to learn words by signing words into her hand. Helen also learned to speak by touching other people's lips and feeling their throats. She also learned to read Braille, a set of raised dots for letters, symbols, and numbers. Later on in life, Helen helped others by becoming an activist. She supported equal rights for women and all people and traveled all over the world to give speeches that encouraged many people to overcome challenges.

36. What sense did Helen NOT lose as a child?

(A) Her touch

(B) Her hearing

(C) Her sight

37. How did Helen help people around the world?

(A) She became Anne's teacher.

(B) She created Braille.

(C) She supported people to overcome challenges.

You finished the reading test.

Do not mark questions 38 and 39.

No test questions on this page

Listening

Part 1 💿 Actual Test 2 #01~06

Fill in the correct circles on your answer sheet.

Let's do an example.

1.

(A)

(B)

(C)

The answer is "B". Fill in "B" on your answer sheet.

Now, you do it.

2.

(A)

(B)

(C)

3.

(A)   (B)   (C)

4.

(A)   (B)   (C)

5.

(A)   (B)   (C)

6.

(A)

(B)

(C)

Part 2 Actual Test 2 #07~15

Listen to a conversation and answer the question.
Fill in the correct circle on your answer sheet.

Let's do an example.

7. **What will the girl probably do next?**

    (A) Talk to her teacher
    (B) Study with the boy
    (C) Go to band practice

    The answer is "C". Fill in "C" on your answer sheet.

    Now, you do it.

---

8. **What promise did the girl's mom make?**

    (A) To pack her swimming bag beforehand.
    (B) To look for her things properly.
    (C) To film her practice.

9. **What does the boy agree to do?**

    (A) Throw away the broken tools.
    (B) Put the paint cans in the recycling bin.
    (C) Help his dad repair the broken tools.

10. **What will the girl wear to Sara's birthday party?**

    (A) A blue dress
    (B) A yellow dress
    (C) A pink dress

11. **What does the girl say she will do?**

    (A)   Make paper ornaments

    (B)   Decorate the Christmas trees

    (C)   Buy Christmas decorations

12. **What will the boy do first?**

    (A)   Paint the birdhouse green

    (B)   Color the birdhouse blue

    (C)   Nail the roof on the birdhouse

13. **Why does the girl want to go to the mall?**

    (A)   She wants to buy a new bag.

    (B)   She needs a new keyboard.

    (C)   She wants to have a look at the new headphones.

14. **What does the girl <u>NOT</u> want to do?**

    (A)   Ride a Ferris wheel

    (B)   Ride a bumper car

    (C)   Have her face painted

15. **What does the girl agree to do?**

    (A)   To practice sports after school

    (B)   To study together in the evening

    (C)   To have dinner at 8

Part 3 Actual Test 2 #16~25

Listen and answer the question.

Fill in the correct circle on your answer sheet.

Let's do an example.

16. **Why did Tom call?**

   (A) To cancel the trip to the beach
   (B) To suggest going to the beach
   (C) To plan a summer vacation

   The answer is "A". Fill in "A" on your answer sheet.

   Now, you do it.

---

17. **Why did Mr. Brown call?**

   (A) To inform her that school will start late
   (B) To make a weather forecast
   (C) To ask about the bus schedule

18. **Where did the boy tell the girl to meet?**

   (A) The library
   (B) The girl's home
   (C) The school auditorium

19. **Why did the girl call?**

   (A) To ask if they can go to the mall to buy a pair of shoes.
   (B) To tell her mom that she's planning to wear her uniform for the piano concert.
   (C) To explain to her mom why she bought the shoes at the mall.

20. What did Sean call about?

   (A)   To tell Arthur how well he's doing

   (B)   To make sure Arthur will visit soon

   (C)   To ask if he wants to spend the summer holidays together

21. Why did Caroline call?

   (A)   To change the coat to another color

   (B)   To see if she could get a larger coat

   (C)   To ask if she could get a refund today

22. Why is Principal Jefferson calling Mr. Lee?

   (A)   He wants to tell him that the award ceremony will be held next week.

   (B)   He wants to invite Mr. Lee to the award ceremony on Thursday.

   (C)   He wants to see if Mr. Lee can be present at the award ceremony.

23. Why did Ria's mom call?

   (A)   To tell her that she is picking up Dad's suit

   (B)   To Tell her that Grandma is with her friends at the mall

   (C)   To ask Ria to remind her dad to pick up his suit

24. What will Isaac do at lunch?

   (A)   Be presented with an MVP award

   (B)   Explain how well he played the match

   (C)   Hear what the coach has to say

25. Why did Penny call?

    (A)   To express how the latest match was the best

    (B)   To show appreciation for being a great role model

    (C)   To say that she has sent an invitation to her match next month

Part 4   Actual Test 2 #26~29

Listen to a story about Lucy and her friends.

26. **What did the three friends do after seeing a long line at the roller coaster?**

    (A)   They waited in line.

    (B)   They decided to go to the arcade zone.

    (C)   They decided to go to the ice rink.

27. **What game did Lucy <u>NOT</u> play at the arcade zone?**

    (A)   Mini-bowling

    (B)   Basketball hoop

    (C)   Air hockey

28. **How did Lucy feel after ice skating for the first time?**

    (A)   Worried

    (B)   Excited

    (C)   Anxious

29. **Where will the three friends probably go next?**

    (A)   To the arcade zone

    (B)   To the cafeteria

    (C)   To the Sailing Cruise

 Actual Test 2 #30~33

Listen to a story about Sara and Sally.

30. **What does Lizzy like to play the most?**

    (A)   Frisbee

    (B)   Fetch

    (C)   Hide-and-seek

31. **How does Lizzy look?**

    (A)   She looked tired from all the running.

    (B)   She looked bored, waiting for Sara to come back.

    (C)   She looked energetic even after all the fetching.

32. **What does Sally notice about Lizzy?**

    (A)   She was panting as she was too excited.

    (B)   She looked like she wanted a drink of water.

    (C)   She seemed to want to play another of her favorite games.

33. **Where did Lizzy go to cool down?**

    (A)   Back home

    (B)   To mom's car

    (C)   To the shade

 Actual Test 2 #34~36

Listen to a teacher talking in a science class.

34. **Why was it hard to see through early telescopes?**

   (A)   The glass was polished by hand.

   (B)   They could only be seen during the day.

   (C)   Only scientists knew how to see clearly through them.

35. **How do telescopes function?**

   (A)   The eyepiece lens minimizes the focused light.

   (B)   The big lenses magnify the focused light.

   (C)   The eyepiece helps people get a clear view of things.

36. **What is <u>NOT</u> a difference between traditional telescopes and radio telescopes?**

   (A)   The size

   (B)   The signals

   (C)   The purpose

Go On

 Actual Test 2 #37~39

Listen to a social studies teacher.

37. **What does the teacher talk about?**

  (A) Inventions that Russia is famous for

  (B) How the weather affects Russia

  (C) The type of food Russia produces

38. **Why have computer games been popular in Russia these days?**

  (A) Because most of the computer games were invented in Russia

  (B) Because they are more fun than chess

  (C) Because it's a great indoor game

39. **Why does the teacher mention Antarctica?**

  (A) To compare Antarctica's size to Russia

  (B) To explain how cold it is in Russia

  (C) To mention an interesting fact about Antarctica

You finished the listening test.

Do not mark questions 40 and 41.

Actual Test 03

Reading

Part 1

Read and find the answer.

Fill in the correct circles on your answer sheet.

Let's do an example.

1. This is a part of my body. It is on my hand. It is one of ten.

    What is it?

    (A) A toe
    (B) A finger
    (C) A foot

    The correct answer is a finger. Fill in "B" on your answer sheet.

---

2. There are eight people coming to your birthday party. You have eight plates but only seven forks and glasses on the table.

    You go back to the cupboard because there _____ forks.

    (A) aren't enough
    (B) are enough
    (C) too many

3. There are some children playing hide-and-seek. Other children are on swings. There are many activities for children to do.

    The children are in a _____.

    (A) swimming pool
    (B) library
    (C) playground

4. You want to go to the movies. You take the bus, but there are so many people in it. Many people are standing close together.

    The bus is _____.

    (A) spacious
    (B) wide
    (C) crowded

5. He was holding his cell phone. A message came, but he didn't know who sent it. It was probably a spam message, so he got rid of it.

    What did he do?

    (A) Opened the message
    (B) Recharged his phone
    (C) Deleted the message

6. The dog is very active. It goes for a walk three times a day. It doesn't rest and wants to play all day.

    The dog is _____.

    (A) hopping
    (B) swinging
    (C) energetic

7. Our class played soccer against another class. The score was 1-1 at half-time. With just 10 seconds to go before the final whistle, our team scored!

    We _____ **them!**

    (A) lost
    (B) beat
    (C) bet

8. It is summer, and the weather is very hot. Many people wear these on their feet in warm weather. They keep your feet cool.

   They are _____.

   (A) necklaces
   (B) sandals
   (C) swimsuits

9. Your English teacher says a word you don't understand. The class is about to finish.

   After class, you _____.

   (A) look at it
   (B) look it up
   (C) look through it

10. He is in a store. He is handing over a bag of fruits to a customer. After that, he receives 5 dollars from the woman and gives the customer a change.

    What is he doing?

    (A) Selling fruit
    (B) Buying fruit
    (C) Collecting fruit

11. A girl is watching a dance show. The dancers are moving their arms and legs in different ways. She gets up and starts trying to copy the dancers.

    She is _____ the dance moves.

    (A) imitating
    (B) folding
    (C) holding

Go On

Reading

Reading

Part 2

Fill in the correct circles on your answer sheet.

Read the poster. Answer questions 12 to 15.

A School Trip to the Local Fire Station

A reminder to all 5th –grade students!

This Wednesday, we will go on a school trip to the local fire station. It will be a great opportunity to learn safety lessons and understand the important roles of firefighters. After our trip, all students will write a short story about the trip. You must include your favorite parts of the visit and what you have learned.

Schedule for Wednesday

10:00 a.m.	Arrival at the Fire Station
10:30 a.m. – 11:30 a.m.	Fire Station Tour
11:30 a.m. – 1:00 p.m.	Fire Safety Lesson
1:00 p.m. – 2:00 p.m.	Lunch
2:00 p.m. – 2:30 p.m.	Group Photo
2:30 p.m.	Back to School

Extra Information

◇ Prepare notebooks and pencils to write down what firefighters are saying.
◇ Wear comfortable clothes and shoes.
◇ Bring a packed lunch.

Go On

12. **Why are students going to the local fire station?**

    (A)   To make a fire safety poster

    (B)   To interview firefighters

    (C)   To learn safety lessons

13. **At what time will the students take a fire station tour?**

    (A)   10:00 a.m.

    (B)   10:30 a.m.

    (C)   11:00 a.m.

14. **What will the students NOT include in their story?**

    (A)   Their favorite firefighter

    (B)   Their favorite parts

    (C)   The things they learned

15. **How long will the fire safety lesson last?**

    (A)   30 minutes

    (B)   1 hour

    (C)   1 hour and 30 minutes

Read the letter. Answer questions 16 and 17.

Hi Grandma!

Did Dad tell you? I won 1st prize at the science fair! I get to choose to go to any museum in the country. I can't decide, though. You know I love animation, trains, and robots, just like you do. I have two tickets so I want you to be my "plus one" to wherever we choose. I did some research, and Comuseum has a day pass for all graphics, comic book exhibits, and technical events, plus giveaways. (You know I love freebies!) Then I looked at M.O.T. (Museum of Technology). They have a day pass with lots of rides and some great exhibits and inventions, but no giveaways. Which one should we go to?

Love,
Grace

---

16. What is <u>NOT</u> true about Grace's prize?

(A) It applies to national museums.

(B) It applies to museums internationally.

(C) It applies to museums in the city.

17. Which Museum would Grace most likely want Grandma to choose?

(A) The one with giveaways

(B) The one with rides

(C) The one with inventions

Read the e-mail. Answer questions 18 and 19.

To: Violet and Ria
From: Sophia
Subject: Pajama Party

I can't wait for our pajama party tomorrow! Have you decided what pajamas you will be wearing? I picked my favorite blue ones, and they're cozy and warm. Make sure to bring your favorite stuffed animal too. We're going to have so much fun!
My mom and I are going to the market to buy snacks and hot chocolate. Do you have any snacks that you want to eat? Please call me and let me know if you do! I already picked a movie for us to watch, but please feel free to bring any movies that you want! I have many board games for us so you don't have to bring anything.

Looking forward to seeing all of you!

Love,
Sophia

18. **Why are Sophia and her mom going to the market?**

   (A)   To rent a movie

   (B)   To buy her pajamas

   (C)   To buy snacks

19. **What will Sophia and her friends NOT do at the party?**

   (A)   Play board games

   (B)   Read books

   (C)   Watch movies

Read the instructions. Answer questions 20 to 22.

Scavenger Hunt!

Today you'll be working with your friends and showing your teamwork. Your mission is to find the items listed below, and the team that finds the most items within the set time will win a prize. After collecting all the items, you must check them off your list and bring it back to your teacher.

Scavenger Hunt List

- Something with wheels
- Something made out of wood
- Something shiny
- Something smooth
- A stick shaped like the letter "Y"
- A clover
- A pinecone
- A red flower

All items can be found within the school campus, including the playground, garden and library. However, you should not go to the parking lot, as there are many cars coming in and out of school. Also, make sure to work in a team by sharing information and communicating with each other.

The time limit is 30 minutes, but 30 more minutes will be given if no team has finished.

** Do not pick up or touch things that look dangerous! Only collect safe things on the list!

20. **What should students do after collecting all the items?**

   (A)   Take pictures

   (B)   Take them home

   (C)   Take them to the teacher

21. **Where should students be looking for the items?**

   (A)   At the local library

   (B)   At the playground

   (C)   At the parking lot

22. **If no team finishes in 30 minutes, how much more time will be given?**

   (A)   Half an hour

   (B)   An hour

   (C)   An hour and thirty minutes

Go On

Read the instructions. Answer questions 23 to 25.

Wonderland Airport

Going to the airport and riding a plane for the first time is very exciting for everyone. To have a great trip, here's what you need to do to make sure everything goes according to plan.

Before Going to the Airport

✓ Check your ticket: Electronic tickets (E-ticket) or paper ticket
✓ Pack your luggage
✓ Check that you have your passport
✓ Make sure to leave at least two hours before your flight

At the Airport

1. Check-in Counter: Give your luggage to the check-in desk.
2. Security: Show your passport to an airline staff member.
3. Before boarding, look at the screen to see which gate it is and check your flight number.
4. Boarding:
   - Line up to show your ticket to a flight attendant.
   - Walk onto the plane.
   - Sit in your seat and buckle your seatbelt.
5. On the plane: Have a look out the window and enjoy the beautiful scenery.
6. Landing: Make sure that you have all your belongings before leaving the plane.
7. Baggage Claim: Follow the signs to collect your baggage.

** Make sure to always have your passport with you!
** Stay aware of the time!

23. When should you <u>NOT</u> leave for the airport?

(A)   An hour early

(B)   Two hours early

(C)   Three hours early

24. What happens at security?

(A)   People check their luggage.

(B)   People show their tickets.

(C)   People show their passports.

25. What should you check for before leaving the plane?

(A)   Check to see if you have all your belongings.

(B)   Buckle your seatbelt.

(C)   Look at the beautiful scenery from the sky.

Reading

Read a story about Jordan and his family. Answer questions 26 to 29.

It was November, as usual, and Jordan and his family were busy preparing for their annual Thanksgiving dinner. The smell of delicious food filled the house, and the family members were preparing to sit around the dinner table.

"Jordan, can you please help me with the napkins? Also, where is your sister? I thought she was laying out the plates," Jordan's mom asked.
"Bella is showing Grandpa that she can finally ride a bike. She's out in the garden with him! As for the napkins and plates, I've already placed them on the dinner table," replied Jordan.
"Thank you! You are always such a help! Now that dinner is almost ready, can you please ask everyone to sit around the dinner table?" asked Jordan's mom as she brought in a big roasted turkey.

Within ten minutes, Jordan's family sat around the dinner table, ready to eat. On the table were many delicious foods, including roast turkey, cranberry sauce, mashed potatoes, gravy, sweet potato casserole, and pumpkin pie.

"Before we eat this wonderful meal, we will go around the table and say what we're thankful for," Jordan's dad said.
Bella raised her hand with excitement. "I would like to start by thanking you, Dad, for teaching me how to ride a bike. Although it was hard at first, you have always been patient with me, so thank you," she said.
"I am proud that you tried so hard, Bella, so well done! How about you, Jordan? Is there anything you are thankful for?" asked Jordan's dad.
"I am thankful to Grandpa and Grandma for always being there for me. You have taught me the importance of trying my best and being kind and honest to people. Also, your encouragement means the world! I will try my best to always think about what you said," replied Jordan.

Jordan's father, beaming with pride, said, "Thank you for saying those kind words to your grandparents. I am very proud of you. What I'm thankful for is this delicious meal! I want to say thank you to my wife and mom for preparing this amazing dinner. Thank you!"

26. What is the story about?

(A)   Thanking Jordan's mom for being a great cook

(B)   Thanking each other for making great food

(C)   Thanking family members for what they have done for each other

27. Why did Jordan's mom thank Jordan?

(A)   For being a great brother and teaching his sister how to ride a bike

(B)   For being a great son and helping her

(C)   For being a great son and helping with the cooking

28. Why did Jordan's family NOT eat right after sitting around the table?

(A)   They wanted to say what they were thankful for.

(B)   They were waiting for more family members to arrive.

(C)   They were waiting for the food to be cooked.

29. How will Jordan try to act in the future?

(A)   He will do what he wants.

(B)   He will try his best to ride a bike.

(C)   He will treat others with kindness and respect.

Go On

Reading

Read a story about Meredith and her dad. Answer questions 30 to 33.

"Dad, I feel so tired, but I can't seem to fall asleep. I felt sleepy in the afternoon, but it's nearly midnight, and my mind is fully awake!" cried Meredith.

"It's normal to experience jet lag, Meredith. Many people go through this process after traveling to different time zones by plane," responded Meredith's dad.

"Different time zones? I think I heard of it before, but what is it exactly?" she asked.

"Good question! As it takes 24 hours for the Earth to complete one full spin, there are 24 different main time zones worldwide. Do you remember the difference between latitude and longitude?" Meredith's dad asked.

"I remember! Latitude lines run horizontally, east to west, and longitude lines run vertically, north to south. I also know about the prime meridian. The 0° longitude line runs from the North Pole to the South Pole. In fact, I learned that it divides the Earth into the Eastern and Western Hemispheres," replied Meredith excitedly.

"I'm so proud! You sure have been concentrating in geography class! There is also something called UTC (Coordinated Universal Time). It is a time standard based on the prime meridian, and it is used as the starting point for the different time zones. Countries around the world use it for timekeeping," explained Dad.

"Wow! So, UTC keeps the world's time standard, but you still haven't explained how people can calculate the time differences," responded Meredith.

"Think of it this way. There are 24 main time zones, and they are roughly 1 hour apart. From the prime meridian, as you move along east, the time increases, and as you move along west, the time decreases," explained Dad.

"That's why it was still afternoon when I arrived in Paris yesterday! I think people would be very confused without UTC," cried Meredith.

"You're right! I'm glad that you know how important time is to us. It helps people travel, work, and communicate with different people all around the world," said Meredith's dad as they went to bed.

30. **What splits the Earth into Eastern and Western hemispheres?**

    (A)   Coordinated Universal Time

    (B)   The prime meridian

    (C)   The different time zones

31. **What is <u>NOT</u> an example mentioned in the passage?**

    (A)   As people move along west, time decreases.

    (B)   It takes twenty-four hours for Earth to rotate fully.

    (C)   Longitude lines run from east to west.

32. **How many hours are the main time zones away from each other?**

    (A)   One hour

    (B)   Two hours

    (C)   Three hours

33. **What is UTC?**

    (A)   It divides the Earth into latitudes and longitudes.

    (B)   It is what helps people get a jet lag.

    (C)   It is what people use to keep time.

Go On

Read about bees. Answer questions 34 and 35.

   Bees are fascinating creatures and are important to the planet and people. There are three kinds of bees: the queen, the workers, and the drones. They all live in a big house called a hive. They all have different jobs, and they work with each other. The queen bee is the most important member of a bee colony. It is the only female bee that can lay eggs. The worker bees are also female, making up most of a colony. They do most of the work, and with them, bees can maintain the organization of their hives. Worker bees make honey by first finding nectar. After sucking up the sweet nectar, they put it in their honey stomachs. Then, they return to their hive and pass the nectar to another bee. When the nectar is mixed with saliva with special enzymes, it changes to honey. Then, they store it in their honeycombs, which are made of wax. There are also the drones. They are all male and larger than worker bees but smaller than the queen bees. Their work is to mate with queen bees to make more bees.

34.   Why is the queen bee the most important member of a bee colony?

   (A)   It is the only bee that makes honey.

   (B)   It is the only bee capable of laying eggs.

   (C)   It is the only bee that can make hives.

35.   What type of bee is male?

   (A)   The queen bees

   (B)   The worker bees

   (C)   The drones

Reading

Read about the environment. Answer questions 36 and 37.

"There is no planet B." People have been polluting the Earth so much that there are major concerns over many environmental problems. Sea levels are rising, glaciers are melting, more animals are becoming endangered, and there is a rise in the global surface temperature. Although what has been done cannot be undone, people must work together to save the Earth and make it a cleaner place for the next generation. Simple acts people can do in their everyday lives will bring **significant** changes in the future. For example, the environment gives us fresh water, so we should be careful to save it and not pollute it. Saving electricity by turning off lights, turning off faucets to save water, and taking public transportation will help reduce carbon dioxide levels. Little acts we can and should do will make a big difference in our future.

36. In line 6, what does **significant** mean?

(A) slight
(B) great
(C) little

37. What environmental problems are **NOT** happening to the Earth?

(A) Glaciers are melting.
(B) More animals are in danger.
(C) The surface temperature is decreasing.

You finished the reading test.

Do not mark questions 38 and 39.

Part 1 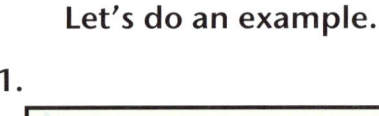 Actual Test 3 #01~06

Fill in the correct circles on your answer sheet.

Let's do an example.

1.

(A)

(B)

(C)

The answer is "C". Fill in "C" on your answer sheet.

Now, you do it.

2.

(A)

(B)

(C)

Test 3

3.

   (A)   (B)   (C)

4.

   (A)   (B)   (C)

5.

   (A)   (B)   (C)

Go On

6.

(A)   (B)   (C)

Listening

Part 2

Actual Test 3 #07~15

Listen to a conversation and answer the question.
Fill in the correct circle on your answer sheet.

Let's do an example.

7. **What is the boy buying?**

(A) Flowers for a model building

(B) A lot of flour to make a model

(C) Flowers, sugar, and salt for the expo

The answer is "B". Fill in "B" on your answer sheet.

Now, you do it.

---

8. **Why does the girl need help washing the top of the car?**

(A) She isn't tall enough.

(B) She wants to see how her dad does it first.

(C) She doesn't like washing the car with water.

9. **What will the boy and his mother do next?**

(A) Go to the market to buy some seeds

(B) Go to the market to buy a large pot

(C) Find a sunny spot to put the tomatoes

10. **What will the girl probably do next?**

(A) Finish all her greens

(B) Finish eating all her lunch

(C) Have cheesecake as a reward

11. **What will the girl probably do next?**

 (A) Cut the lemons into slices

 (B) Drink lemonade

 (C) Clean the kitchen

12. **What will the boy get for his parents' anniversary?**

 (A) Pajamas

 (B) Flowers

 (C) Cake

13. **What is the conversation about?**

 (A) Why the boy wants to go early

 (B) Why the bookstore is opening early

 (C) Why the book sold out early

14. **What will the boy and his dad have for dinner?**

 (A) Chinese

 (B) Salad with chicken

 (C) Tacos

15. **What will the children do next?**

 (A) Return the milk

 (B) Get a loaf of bread

 (C) Change the egg carton

Part 3   Actual Test 3 #16~25

Listen and answer the question.

Fill in the correct circle on your answer sheet.

Let's do an example.

16. What did Principal Cindy ask the students?

    (A)   Not to bring a lunch box to the field trip

    (B)   To meet in front of the school at 8:30 a.m. on Friday

    (C)   To be on their best behavior on the field trip

The answer is "C". Fill in "C" on your answer sheet.

Now, you do it.

---

17. Why did Bella's mom call?

    (A)   To ask Bella about her thoughts on an upcoming debate

    (B)   To see if Bella wants to start learning French

    (C)   To tell Bella to call her French teacher

18. What will Aaron probably do?

    (A)   Tell Sara about an available spot

    (B)   Get back to Sara and let her know if he can make it

    (C)   Thank Sara for the Saturday tickets to the music festival

19. What did Grace's mom NOT ask her to do?

    (A)   To run the washing machine

    (B)   To sort and fold the clothes

    (C)   To get a nutritious meal for dinner

20. Why did the principal call?

(A)   She is asking about the kind of work she can do as a volunteer.

(B)   She wants to know if Mrs. Woods can meet to go over a problem.

(C)   She is interested in discussing the new volunteer opportunities for this year.

21. Why did Olivia's grandad call?

(A)   He wants to go jogging with her.

(B)   He wanted to ask if Olivia is running every morning.

(C)   He was wondering if Olivia needed help with her tests.

22. What will Jin's aunt do next?

(A)   Head over to Jin's school.

(B)   Wait for Jin to call.

(C)   Wait in front of the school.

23. Why did Meredith call her dad?

(A)   She needs help remembering her lines for her presentation.

(B)   She doesn't know how to download the pictures she wants.

(C)   She doesn't know how to place pictures in her presentation slides.

24. What will Vince do next?

(A)   Go to the lost-and-found

(B)   Go to swim practice

(C)   Go to the main office

25. Why did Chloe call Mrs. Gibson?

    (A)   To tell her about the great news that the show will start soon

    (B)   To show appreciation for all her encouragement

    (C)   To tell her how eager she is to go and watch the musical

Part 4 Actual Test 3 #26~29

Listen to a story about David and Diane.

26. Why couldn't Diane take a picture of the UFO?

(A) She couldn't see it clearly.

(B) It passed by in the blink of an eye.

(C) Her sister Lily didn't tell her quickly enough.

27. How do Diane and David spend most of their time together?

(A) They eat ice cream.

(B) They debate about extraterrestrials.

(C) They gaze at the sky and think about what exists beyond Earth.

28. Why doesn't David believe that aliens exist?

(A) He has seen a UFO but not aliens.

(B) He hasn't seen one for himself.

(C) He assumes that Diane is always joking.

29. Why did Diane roll her eyes?

(A) She has had this conversation with David before.

(B) She explained too many times that she had seen a UFO.

(C) She doesn't understand why David doesn't believe in scientific facts.

 Actual Test 3 #30~33

Listen to a teacher talking about an adventurer.

30. Why is Amelia a well-known pilot?

   (A)   She broke many records as a pilot.

   (B)   She was the first woman pilot of her time.

   (C)   She is famous for flying around the world.

31. What inspired her to become a pilot?

   (A)   Her dad encouraged her because he was a pilot.

   (B)   Her love for airplanes was love at first sight.

   (C)   Her first flight in an airplane seemed like fate.

32. What is true about Amelia?

   (A)   In 1932, she made her final flight over the Pacific Ocean.

   (B)   In 1932, she made her first solo flight across the Atlantic.

   (C)   In 1932, she was the first woman to fly across the Atlantic as part of a crew.

33. What does <u>NOT</u> describe Amelia in the passage?

   (A)   Many people look up to her for many reasons.

   (B)   The radio connection went silent on her final flight.

   (C)   Fred Noonan was her navigator and husband.

 Actual Test 3 #34~36

Listen to a teacher talking in a social studies class.

34. **Why did artists in the past use white bread?**

   (A)   They used it to correct their mistakes.

   (B)   It was a common material to use with a paintbrush.

   (C)   Bread was a cheap option to use when erasing something.

35. **What kind of bread can people use to clean their houses?**

   (A)   Fresh white bread

   (B)   Warm brown bread

   (C)   Dry white bread

36. **What does <u>NOT</u> describe how bread can be used?**

   (A)   It can be used instead of a plate.

   (B)   Artists used it to create paintings.

   (C)   People can use it to wipe off dust.

Go On

 Actual Test 3 #37~39

Listen to a teacher talking in a science class.

37. What is pollination?

(A)   It helps flowers to stay colorful.

(B)   It serves as a way to make carbon dioxide.

(C)   It supports flowers to make new plants.

38. What is <u>NOT</u> the role of stems?

(A)   They prevent flowers from falling over.

(B)   They deliver nutrients to flowers.

(C)   They produce a type of sugar.

39. What do leaves do?

(A)   They create food by using sunlight.

(B)   They take in nutrients from the soil.

(C)   They serve as anchors for flowers.

You finished the listening test.

Do not mark questions 40 and 41.

EXAMPLE

YES	NO	NO	NO	NO
Ⓐ Ⓑ ●	Ⓐ Ⓑ Ⓒ̷	Ⓐ Ⓑ ☒	Ⓐ Ⓑ̲ Ⓒ	Ⓐ Ⓑ Ⓒ

Print your name in your first language:

Test Center Name:

Form Code:

Test Date:

SCHOOL USE ONLY
Is Consent Form on file? ○ Yes ○ No

1. NAME: Print your name. Using one box for each letter, first print your Given (first) name, then your Family (last) name. Below each box, use a No. 2 pencil and fill in the circle matching the same letter.

GIVEN (FIRST) NAME   FAMILY (LAST) NAME

2. STUDENT NUMBER — Start here

3. DATE OF BIRTH

Month	Day	Year
○ Jan		
○ Feb		
○ Mar		
○ Apr		
○ May		
○ Jun		
○ Jul		
○ Aug		
○ Sep		
○ Oct		
○ Nov		
○ Dec		

4. GENDER

BOY ○

GIRL ○

5. COUNTRY CODE

6. LANGUAGE CODE

7. At my school I am in:
○ Grade 1
○ Grade 2
○ Grade 3
○ Grade 4
○ Grade 5
○ Grade 6
○ Grade 7
○ Grade 8
○ Grade 9
○ Other

8. I have studied English for:
○ 1 year or less
○ 2 years
○ 3 years
○ 4 years
○ 5 years
○ 6 years or more

9. What test(s) have you taken before?
○ TOEFL Primary Step 1
○ TOEFL Primary Step 2
○ Both
○ None

10. GROUP CODE (if assigned)

11. CODE SETS (if assigned)

CODE SET 1   CODE SET 2   CODE SET 3

PAGE 1

참고서 사용하세요.

Reading

1.	(A)	(B)	(C)
2.	(A)	(B)	(C)
3.	(A)	(B)	(C)
4.	(A)	(B)	(C)
5.	(A)	(B)	(C)
6.	(A)	(B)	(C)
7.	(A)	(B)	(C)
8.	(A)	(B)	(C)
9.	(A)	(B)	(C)
10.	(A)	(B)	(C)
11.	(A)	(B)	(C)
12.	(A)	(B)	(C)
13.	(A)	(B)	(C)

14.	(A)	(B)	(C)
15.	(A)	(B)	(C)
16.	(A)	(B)	(C)
17.	(A)	(B)	(C)
18.	(A)	(B)	(C)
19.	(A)	(B)	(C)
20.	(A)	(B)	(C)
21.	(A)	(B)	(C)
22.	(A)	(B)	(C)
23.	(A)	(B)	(C)
24.	(A)	(B)	(C)
25.	(A)	(B)	(C)
26.	(A)	(B)	(C)

27.	(A)	(B)	(C)
28.	(A)	(B)	(C)
29.	(A)	(B)	(C)
30.	(A)	(B)	(C)
31.	(A)	(B)	(C)
32.	(A)	(B)	(C)
33.	(A)	(B)	(C)
34.	(A)	(B)	(C)
35.	(A)	(B)	(C)
36.	(A)	(B)	(C)
37.	(A)	(B)	(C)
38.	(A)	(B)	(C)
39.	(A)	(B)	(C)

Listening

1.	(A)	(B)	(C)
2.	(A)	(B)	(C)
3.	(A)	(B)	(C)
4.	(A)	(B)	(C)
5.	(A)	(B)	(C)
6.	(A)	(B)	(C)
7.	(A)	(B)	(C)
8.	(A)	(B)	(C)
9.	(A)	(B)	(C)
10.	(A)	(B)	(C)
11.	(A)	(B)	(C)
12.	(A)	(B)	(C)
13.	(A)	(B)	(C)
14.	(A)	(B)	(C)

15.	(A)	(B)	(C)
16.	(A)	(B)	(C)
17.	(A)	(B)	(C)
18.	(A)	(B)	(C)
19.	(A)	(B)	(C)
20.	(A)	(B)	(C)
21.	(A)	(B)	(C)
22.	(A)	(B)	(C)
23.	(A)	(B)	(C)
24.	(A)	(B)	(C)
25.	(A)	(B)	(C)
26.	(A)	(B)	(C)
27.	(A)	(B)	(C)
28.	(A)	(B)	(C)

29.	(A)	(B)	(C)
30.	(A)	(B)	(C)
31.	(A)	(B)	(C)
32.	(A)	(B)	(C)
33.	(A)	(B)	(C)
34.	(A)	(B)	(C)
35.	(A)	(B)	(C)
36.	(A)	(B)	(C)
37.	(A)	(B)	(C)
38.	(A)	(B)	(C)
39.	(A)	(B)	(C)
40.	(A)	(B)	(C)
41.	(A)	(B)	(C)

Print your name in your first language:

Test Center Name:

Form Code:

Test Date:

1. **NAME:** Print your name. Using one box for each letter, first print your Given (first) name, then your Family (last) name. Below each box, use a No. 2 pencil and fill in the circle matching the same letter.

GIVEN (FIRST) NAME

FAMILY (LAST) NAME

2. **STUDENT NUMBER**
→ **Start here**

3. **DATE OF BIRTH**

Month	Day	Year
◯ Jan		
◯ Feb		
◯ Mar		
◯ Apr		
◯ May		
◯ Jun		
◯ Jul		
◯ Aug		
◯ Sep		
◯ Oct		
◯ Nov		
◯ Dec		

4. **GENDER**

BOY ◯

GIRL ◯

5. **COUNTRY CODE**

6. **LANGUAGE CODE**

7. At my school I am in:
- ◯ Grade 1
- ◯ Grade 2
- ◯ Grade 3
- ◯ Grade 4
- ◯ Grade 5
- ◯ Grade 6
- ◯ Grade 7
- ◯ Grade 8
- ◯ Grade 9
- ◯ Other

8. I have studied English for:
- ◯ 1 year or less
- ◯ 2 years
- ◯ 3 years
- ◯ 4 years
- ◯ 5 years
- ◯ 6 years or more

9. What test(s) have you taken before?
- ◯ TOEFL Primary Step 1
- ◯ TOEFL Primary Step 2
- ◯ Both
- ◯ None

10. **GROUP CODE** (if assigned)

11. **CODE SETS** (if assigned)

CODE SET 1	CODE SET 2	CODE SET 3

PAGE 1

참가자 사용하세요.

Reading

1.	Ⓐ Ⓑ Ⓒ	14.	Ⓐ Ⓑ Ⓒ	27.	Ⓐ Ⓑ Ⓒ
2.	Ⓐ Ⓑ Ⓒ	15.	Ⓐ Ⓑ Ⓒ	28.	Ⓐ Ⓑ Ⓒ
3.	Ⓐ Ⓑ Ⓒ	16.	Ⓐ Ⓑ Ⓒ	29.	Ⓐ Ⓑ Ⓒ
4.	Ⓐ Ⓑ Ⓒ	17.	Ⓐ Ⓑ Ⓒ	30.	Ⓐ Ⓑ Ⓒ
5.	Ⓐ Ⓑ Ⓒ	18.	Ⓐ Ⓑ Ⓒ	31.	Ⓐ Ⓑ Ⓒ
6.	Ⓐ Ⓑ Ⓒ	19.	Ⓐ Ⓑ Ⓒ	32.	Ⓐ Ⓑ Ⓒ
7.	Ⓐ Ⓑ Ⓒ	20.	Ⓐ Ⓑ Ⓒ	33.	Ⓐ Ⓑ Ⓒ
8.	Ⓐ Ⓑ Ⓒ	21.	Ⓐ Ⓑ Ⓒ	34.	Ⓐ Ⓑ Ⓒ
9.	Ⓐ Ⓑ Ⓒ	22.	Ⓐ Ⓑ Ⓒ	35.	Ⓐ Ⓑ Ⓒ
10.	Ⓐ Ⓑ Ⓒ	23.	Ⓐ Ⓑ Ⓒ	36.	Ⓐ Ⓑ Ⓒ
11.	Ⓐ Ⓑ Ⓒ	24.	Ⓐ Ⓑ Ⓒ	37.	Ⓐ Ⓑ Ⓒ
12.	Ⓐ Ⓑ Ⓒ	25.	Ⓐ Ⓑ Ⓒ	38.	Ⓐ Ⓑ Ⓒ
13.	Ⓐ Ⓑ Ⓒ	26.	Ⓐ Ⓑ Ⓒ	39.	Ⓐ Ⓑ Ⓒ

Listening

1.	Ⓐ Ⓑ Ⓒ	15.	Ⓐ Ⓑ Ⓒ	29.	Ⓐ Ⓑ Ⓒ
2.	Ⓐ Ⓑ Ⓒ	16.	Ⓐ Ⓑ Ⓒ	30.	Ⓐ Ⓑ Ⓒ
3.	Ⓐ Ⓑ Ⓒ	17.	Ⓐ Ⓑ Ⓒ	31.	Ⓐ Ⓑ Ⓒ
4.	Ⓐ Ⓑ Ⓒ	18.	Ⓐ Ⓑ Ⓒ	32.	Ⓐ Ⓑ Ⓒ
5.	Ⓐ Ⓑ Ⓒ	19.	Ⓐ Ⓑ Ⓒ	33.	Ⓐ Ⓑ Ⓒ
6.	Ⓐ Ⓑ Ⓒ	20.	Ⓐ Ⓑ Ⓒ	34.	Ⓐ Ⓑ Ⓒ
7.	Ⓐ Ⓑ Ⓒ	21.	Ⓐ Ⓑ Ⓒ	35.	Ⓐ Ⓑ Ⓒ
8.	Ⓐ Ⓑ Ⓒ	22.	Ⓐ Ⓑ Ⓒ	36.	Ⓐ Ⓑ Ⓒ
9.	Ⓐ Ⓑ Ⓒ	23.	Ⓐ Ⓑ Ⓒ	37.	Ⓐ Ⓑ Ⓒ
10.	Ⓐ Ⓑ Ⓒ	24.	Ⓐ Ⓑ Ⓒ	38.	Ⓐ Ⓑ Ⓒ
11.	Ⓐ Ⓑ Ⓒ	25.	Ⓐ Ⓑ Ⓒ	39.	Ⓐ Ⓑ Ⓒ
12.	Ⓐ Ⓑ Ⓒ	26.	Ⓐ Ⓑ Ⓒ	40.	Ⓐ Ⓑ Ⓒ
13.	Ⓐ Ⓑ Ⓒ	27.	Ⓐ Ⓑ Ⓒ	41.	Ⓐ Ⓑ Ⓒ
14.	Ⓐ Ⓑ Ⓒ	28.	Ⓐ Ⓑ Ⓒ		

EXAMPLE

YES	NO	NO	NO	NO
Ⓐ Ⓑ ●	Ⓐ Ⓑ Ⓒ✓	Ⓐ Ⓑ Ⓧ	Ⓐ Ⓑ Ⓒ	Ⓐ Ⓑ Ⓒ

Print your name in your first language:

Test Center Name:

Form Code:

Test Date:

SCHOOL USE ONLY
Is Consent Form on file? ◯ Yes ◯ No

1. **NAME:** Print your name. Using one box for each letter, first print your Given (first) name, then your Family (last) name. Below each box, use a No. 2 pencil and fill in the circle matching the same letter.

GIVEN (FIRST) NAME

FAMILY (LAST) NAME

2. **STUDENT NUMBER** — Start here

3. **DATE OF BIRTH**

Month	Day	Year
◯ Jan		
◯ Feb		
◯ Mar		
◯ Apr		
◯ May		
◯ Jun		
◯ Jul		
◯ Aug		
◯ Sep		
◯ Oct		
◯ Nov		
◯ Dec		

4. **GENDER**

BOY ◯

GIRL ◯

5. **COUNTRY CODE**

6. **LANGUAGE CODE**

7. At my school I am in:
- ◯ Grade 1
- ◯ Grade 2
- ◯ Grade 3
- ◯ Grade 4
- ◯ Grade 5
- ◯ Grade 6
- ◯ Grade 7
- ◯ Grade 8
- ◯ Grade 9
- ◯ Other

8. I have studied English for:
- ◯ 1 year or less
- ◯ 2 years
- ◯ 3 years
- ◯ 4 years
- ◯ 5 years
- ◯ 6 years or more

9. What test(s) have you taken before?
- ◯ TOEFL Primary Step 1
- ◯ TOEFL Primary Step 2
- ◯ Both
- ◯ None

10. **GROUP CODE** (if assigned)

11. **CODE SETS** (if assigned)

CODE SET 1	CODE SET 2	CODE SET 3

PAGE 1

Reading

1. Ⓐ Ⓑ Ⓒ	14. Ⓐ Ⓑ Ⓒ	27. Ⓐ Ⓑ Ⓒ
2. Ⓐ Ⓑ Ⓒ	15. Ⓐ Ⓑ Ⓒ	28. Ⓐ Ⓑ Ⓒ
3. Ⓐ Ⓑ Ⓒ	16. Ⓐ Ⓑ Ⓒ	29. Ⓐ Ⓑ Ⓒ
4. Ⓐ Ⓑ Ⓒ	17. Ⓐ Ⓑ Ⓒ	30. Ⓐ Ⓑ Ⓒ
5. Ⓐ Ⓑ Ⓒ	18. Ⓐ Ⓑ Ⓒ	31. Ⓐ Ⓑ Ⓒ
6. Ⓐ Ⓑ Ⓒ	19. Ⓐ Ⓑ Ⓒ	32. Ⓐ Ⓑ Ⓒ
7. Ⓐ Ⓑ Ⓒ	20. Ⓐ Ⓑ Ⓒ	33. Ⓐ Ⓑ Ⓒ
8. Ⓐ Ⓑ Ⓒ	21. Ⓐ Ⓑ Ⓒ	34. Ⓐ Ⓑ Ⓒ
9. Ⓐ Ⓑ Ⓒ	22. Ⓐ Ⓑ Ⓒ	35. Ⓐ Ⓑ Ⓒ
10. Ⓐ Ⓑ Ⓒ	23. Ⓐ Ⓑ Ⓒ	36. Ⓐ Ⓑ Ⓒ
11. Ⓐ Ⓑ Ⓒ	24. Ⓐ Ⓑ Ⓒ	37. Ⓐ Ⓑ Ⓒ
12. Ⓐ Ⓑ Ⓒ	25. Ⓐ Ⓑ Ⓒ	38. Ⓐ Ⓑ Ⓒ
13. Ⓐ Ⓑ Ⓒ	26. Ⓐ Ⓑ Ⓒ	39. Ⓐ Ⓑ Ⓒ

Listening

1. Ⓐ Ⓑ Ⓒ	15. Ⓐ Ⓑ Ⓒ	29. Ⓐ Ⓑ Ⓒ
2. Ⓐ Ⓑ Ⓒ	16. Ⓐ Ⓑ Ⓒ	30. Ⓐ Ⓑ Ⓒ
3. Ⓐ Ⓑ Ⓒ	17. Ⓐ Ⓑ Ⓒ	31. Ⓐ Ⓑ Ⓒ
4. Ⓐ Ⓑ Ⓒ	18. Ⓐ Ⓑ Ⓒ	32. Ⓐ Ⓑ Ⓒ
5. Ⓐ Ⓑ Ⓒ	19. Ⓐ Ⓑ Ⓒ	33. Ⓐ Ⓑ Ⓒ
6. Ⓐ Ⓑ Ⓒ	20. Ⓐ Ⓑ Ⓒ	34. Ⓐ Ⓑ Ⓒ
7. Ⓐ Ⓑ Ⓒ	21. Ⓐ Ⓑ Ⓒ	35. Ⓐ Ⓑ Ⓒ
8. Ⓐ Ⓑ Ⓒ	22. Ⓐ Ⓑ Ⓒ	36. Ⓐ Ⓑ Ⓒ
9. Ⓐ Ⓑ Ⓒ	23. Ⓐ Ⓑ Ⓒ	37. Ⓐ Ⓑ Ⓒ
10. Ⓐ Ⓑ Ⓒ	24. Ⓐ Ⓑ Ⓒ	38. Ⓐ Ⓑ Ⓒ
11. Ⓐ Ⓑ Ⓒ	25. Ⓐ Ⓑ Ⓒ	39. Ⓐ Ⓑ Ⓒ
12. Ⓐ Ⓑ Ⓒ	26. Ⓐ Ⓑ Ⓒ	40. Ⓐ Ⓑ Ⓒ
13. Ⓐ Ⓑ Ⓒ	27. Ⓐ Ⓑ Ⓒ	41. Ⓐ Ⓑ Ⓒ
14. Ⓐ Ⓑ Ⓒ	28. Ⓐ Ⓑ Ⓒ	

Memo

Memo

Memo

Memo

Ace the TOEFL Primary

TOEFL Primary

Step 2 (Reading & Listening)

Answer Key

Ace the
TOEFL Primary

Step 2 (Reading & Listening)

Answer Key

Reading

1 (B)	**2** (A)	**3** (C)	**4** (A)
5 (B)	**6** (B)	**7** (A)	**8** (B)
9 (C)	**10** (A)	**11** (C)	**12** (C)
13 (C)	**14** (B)	**15** (A)	**16** (B)
17 (B)	**18** (C)	**19** (C)	**20** (C)
21 (B)	**22** (A)	**23** (B)	**24** (C)
25 (B)	**26** (C)	**27** (B)	**28** (A)
29 (B)	**30** (C)	**31** (C)	**32** (B)
33 (C)	**34** (B)	**35** (A)	**36** (B)
37 (C)			

Part 1.

1. 이것은 여러 가지 방법으로 사용되고, 전 세계 사람들이 이것을 사용합니다. 이것은 다양한 재료로 만들어지는데, 재료에 따라 이것이 내는 소리에 영향을 줍니다. 사람들이 소리를 내려면 그것을 흔들어야 합니다. 이것은 _____ 이다.

(A) 리본
(B) 종
(C) 부채

2. 당신에게는 자가 없습니다. 깔끔한 선을 그으려면 자가 필요합니다. 당신은 자를 가진 친구를 발견합니다. 당신은 친구에게서 자를 _____ 합니다.

(A) 빌리다
(B) 빌려주다
(C) 보내다

3. 이것은 재킷, 가방 또는 장갑으로 만들 수 있는 동물의 가죽입니다. 이것은 소파나 자동차 좌석을 덮는 데 사용할 수 있습니다.

(A) 면
(B) 양털
(C) 가죽

4. 당신은 무대 위에 서 있습니다. 학교에서 열심히 노력한 결과로 트로피와 상장을 받습니다. 사람들이 박수를 보냅니다.
당신은 _____.

(A) 자랑스럽다
(B) 혼란스럽다
(C) 불안하다

5. 당신은 많은 노력과 시간을 투자합니다. 더 잘하기 위해 연습을 반복합니다. 더 나아지기 위해서 최선을 다합니다. 당신의 실력은 _____ 될 것입니다.

(A) 하락
(B) 향상
(C) 감소

6. 이것들은 0부터 9까지의 숫자를 가지고 있습니다. 이것으로 게임을 하거나 친구에게 전화를 걸 수는 없지만, 더하기, 빼기, 곱하기, 나누기를 할 수 있습니다. 이것은 공부에 도움이 됩니다. 이것은 무엇인가요?

(A) 카메라
(B) 계산기
(C) 복사기

7. 사람들이 큰 테이블에 둘러앉아 있습니다. 그들은 프리젠테이션을 보고 있습니다. 그들은 일하고 있는 것처럼 보입니다. 사람들은 _____ 하고 있습니다.

(A) 소통
(B) 요리
(C) 수집

8. 당신은 최근 수영 동호회에 가입했습니다. 물속에서 숨을 참는 법을 배우고, 발차기를 연습하며, 간단한 영법을 위한 팔동작을 배우고 있습니다. 당신은 매일 _____ 발전하고 있습니다.

(A) 겁을 먹으며
(B) 기초를 배우며
(C) 하고 싶은 말을 참으며

9. 동생이 생일 파티를 합니다. 동생을 도와 생일 초대장을 씁니다. 초대장을 모두 작성한 후 보내려고 합니다. 당신은 그것들을 _____ 에 넣습니다.

(A) 이미지
(B) 화살표
(C) 봉투

10. 많은 사람이 여기서 공부합니다. 이곳들 중 어떤 곳은 작고, 어떤 곳은 매우 큽니다. 이곳에는 책상, 의자, 책들이 있습니다. 이곳은 어디일까요?

(A) 학교
(B) 사무실 건물
(C) 병원

Part 2.

[11-14] 아래를 읽고, 11-14번 질문에 답하세요.

> South Bradford School
> 제과 판매 자선 모금 행사
>
> 이번 주말, 우리 학교 학생들이 자선기금을 모금합니다.

우리 사회를 더 나은 곳으로 만드는데 함께해 주세요!

일시:
• 토요일 정오~오후 6시
• 일요일 오전 9시~정오

세부사항:
모든 학생은 아래의 디저트 중 하나 이상을 가져와야 합니다.
외부 음식이나 음료는 허용되지 않습니다.

케이크
당근 케이크 $7.00
사과 케이크 $8.00
치즈 케이크 $6.50

컵케이크
레몬 $3.00
솔티드 캐러멜 $4.50
딸기 $2.50

도넛
바닐라 $1.50
초콜릿 $2.00
슈거-글레이즈 $3.50

11. 학생들은 모금 행사에 무엇을 가져와야 합니까?

(A) 프라이드치킨
(B) 레모네이드
(C) 치즈케이크

12. 일요일에는 빵 판매 행사가 몇 시에 끝납니까?

(A) 오후 6시
(B) 오후 4시
(C) 오후 12시

13. 가장 비싼 케이크는 무엇입니까?

(A) 치즈 케이크
(B) 당근 케이크
(C) 사과 케이크

14. 학교는 왜 빵 판매 행사를 합니까?

(A) 학생들에게 빵 굽는 법을 가르치기 위해
(B) 자선 기금을 모으기 위해
(C) 지역 행사 Bake Sale에서 우승하기 위해

[15-16] 편지를 읽고, 15-16번 질문에 답하세요.

Aileen에게,

즐거운 겨울 방학 보내고 있지? 난 밴쿠버에서 멋진 시간을 보내고 있어. 3일이 지났지만 너무 즐거웠어. 가족과 함께 Stanley Park에 갔는데, 거기 세계적으로 유명한 수족관이 있더라고. 하지만 지금까지 가장 좋았던 것은 Robson Square 야외 아이스링크에서 스케이트를

타는 것이었어.
곧 크리스마스라서, 오늘 밤 가족과 함께 큰 크리스마스 마켓에 갈 계획이야. 아름답게 반짝이는 불빛들을 보고, 여러 음식을 맛보고, 따뜻한 핫초코를 마실 생각에 너무 기대돼. 아빠 말로는 커다란 빨간 리본이 달린 엄청나게 큰 크리스마스트리도 있대. 다음 편지에서 꼭 더 많은 사진을 보낼게.

사랑을 담아
Agnes

15. Agnes가 여행에서 가장 좋아한 것은 무엇입니까?

(A) 야외 아이스링크에서 스케이트 타기
(B) 동물 사진 찍기
(C) 핫초코 마시기

16. Agnes는 오늘 밤 무엇을 하기를 기대하고 있습니까?

(A) 큰 크리스마스트리 장식하기
(B) 여러 음식 맛보기
(C) 세계적으로 유명한 수족관 방문하기

[17-18] 이메일을 읽고, 17-18번 질문에 답하세요.

받는 사람: Spencer 선생님
보낸 사람: Emma
제목: 졸업

Spencer 선생님께,

내일 졸업한다는 것이 믿기지 않습니다. Louisville School에서 정말 많은 것을 배웠습니다. 훌륭한 선생님이 되어 주셔서 정말 감사드립니다. 선생님께서 저에게 노력의 중요성을 가르쳐 주셨던 것이 모든 수업에서 도움이 되었습니다. 모든 학생이 존중받는다고 느낄 수 있도록 가르치려고 애써 주셔서 감사드립니다. 선생님께서는 인내심과 유머를 가지고 저와 많은 학생들이 최선을 다할 수 있도록 이끌어 주셨습니다. 늘 저를 격려해 주셔서 다시 한번 감사드립니다.

존경을 담아,
Emma 드림

17. Emma가 Spencer 선생님께 이메일을 쓴 이유는 무엇입니까?

(A) 졸업 파티에 대해 감사하기 위해
(B) 훌륭한 선생님이 되어 주신 것에 감사하기 위해
(C) 학생들을 가르치는 것을 도와준 것에 감사하기 위해

18. Emma가 Spencer 선생님께 배운 것이 <u>아닌</u> 것은 무엇입니까?

(A) 노력
(B) 최선을 다하는 태도
(C) 유머

받는 사람: Sean
보낸 사람: Ian
제목: 부모님 결혼기념일

Sean, 좋은 한 주 보내고 있지? 이번 주말 부모님 결혼기념일에 대한 자세한 사항을 알려 주려고 해. 부모님이 가장 좋아하는 이탈리아 레스토랑을 오후 7시로 예약했고, 레스토랑에 엄마가 가장 좋아하는 레몬 케이크를 준비해달라고 요청해 놨어. 이제 토요일에 Leo 삼촌과 Julie 숙모를 기차역에서 모셔 오기만 하면 돼.
나는 그날 오후 늦게 축구 연습이 있어서 혹시 네가 Leo 삼촌과 Julie 숙모를 기차역에서 모시고 올 수 있겠어? 두 분은 오후 5시경에 도착하실 예정이야. 두 분과 함께 바로 레스토랑으로 오면 될 것 같아.

바로 연락해 줘!

Ian 보냄

19. Ian이 Sean에게 부탁한 것은 무엇입니까?

(A) 이탈리아 식당 예약하기
(B) 레몬 케이크 구입하기
(C) Leo 삼촌과 Julie 숙모를 기차역에서 모셔 오기

20. Ian은 레스토랑을 몇 시로 예약했습니까?

(A) 오후 5시
(B) 오후 6시
(C) 오후 7시

학생 여러분께,

제가 중국으로 1년간 여행을 떠나게 되어 앞으로 1년 동안 수업을 쉬게 되었다는 소식을 전하고자 이 편지를 씁니다. 여러분 한명 한명이 그리울 거예요. 여러분은 모두 매우 재능 있고 똑똑한 학생들입니다. 올해 여러분을 가르치면서 매우 즐거운 시간을 보냈답니다. 저는 여러분에게서 많은 것을 배웠고, 여러분도 저에게서 무언가를 배울 수 있었기를 바랍니다. 혹시 저에게 필요한 것이 있거나 저에게 연락할 일이 있으면 언제든지 이메일 보내주세요. 가능한 한 빨리 답장 할게요.

진심을 담아,
Richardson 선생님 보냄

21. Richardson 선생님은 얼마나 오래 여행을 할 예정입니까?

(A) 1개월
(B) 1년
(C) 한 학기

22. Richardson 선생님에 대한 사실이 <u>아닌</u> 것은 무엇입니까?

(A) 학생들은 선생님에게 전화로 연락할 수 있다.

(B) 학생들로부터 많은 것을 배웠다.
(C) 모든 학생을 그리워할 것이다.

나만의 슈퍼히어로 만들기

슈퍼히어로는 저마다 다른 힘과 독특한 특징을 가지며, 특별한 옷을 입기도 합니다. 오늘은 여러분만의 특별한 슈퍼히어로를 직접 만들어 볼 거예요! 그들은 여러분이 상상하는 모든 것이 될 수 있습니다.

지시 사항:
1. 여러분의 슈퍼히어로가 어떤 능력이나 기술을 가질지 상상해 봅니다.
2. 슈퍼히어로가 어떤 모습일지 그려 봅니다.
3. 어떤 옷을 입을지 정합니다.
4. 슈퍼히어로의 옷을 그리고, 색칠합니다.
   - 특별한 능력을 나타내는 상징을 꼭 그려 넣습니다.
   - 어떤 색을 입을지 생각합니다. 선택한 색깔과 성격이 잘 어울리도록 해보세요.
5. 여러분의 슈퍼히어로에 대해 발표할 준비를 합니다.
   - 이름을 지어 주세요!
   - 여러분의 슈퍼히어로가 특별한 이유는 무엇인가요?
   - 여러분의 슈퍼히어로는 어떻게 다른 사람을 돕나요?

23. 슈퍼히어로의 의상에 상징을 추가해야 하는 이유는 무엇입니까?

(A) 그들의 키를 설명하기 위해
(B) 그들의 특별한 능력을 설명하기 위해
(C) 그들이 얼마나 빠른지 설명하기 위해

24. 슈퍼히어로 의상의 색깔을 생각해야 하는 이유는 무엇입니까?

(A) 그들이 얼마나 매력적인지 보여주기 위해
(B) 다른 슈퍼히어로를 돕기 위해
(C) 그들이 어떤 성격을 가졌는지 보여주기 위해

25. 5단계에서 '발표'는 무엇을 의미합니까?

(A) 듣기
(B) 말하기
(C) 보기

Jenny의 가족이 차를 타고 작은 비숑 프리제 강아지인 Mia를 데리러 가는 중입니다. 그들은 Mia를 새로운 가족으로 맞이하는 것에 대한 책임에 대해 이야기합니다.
Jenny의 엄마가 말했습니다. "Jenny, Mia를 집으로 데려오는 것이 매우 신나겠지만, 우리 모두가 지켜야 할 책임에 대해서도 이야기해 보자."
Jenny가 대답했습니다. "네, 엄마! 강아지를 돌보는 법에 대한 영상도 보고 책도 읽었어요. 유용한 정보가 정말 많아서 앞으로도 이렇게 계속 배우고 싶어요."
Jenny의 아빠가 물었습니다. "그런 노력을 했다니 기특하구나. 어떤 것을 배웠는지 말해볼래?"

Jenny가 답했습니다. "우선, Mia는 하루에 최소 두 번은 먹어야 해요. 또한 개들은 물을 많이 마시기 때문에 항상 깨끗한 물이 필요해요."

Jenny의 엄마가 말했습니다. "대단하구나! 개들은 물을 많이 마셔야 해. 사람처럼 말이지. 개들도 우리처럼 수분을 충분히 섭취해야 한단다."

Jenny가 신이 나서 말했습니다. "Mia는 다른 개들보다 물을 더 많이 마실 거예요. 제가 매일 오랜 산책을 시킬 거거든요! 평일에는 학교 끝나고 바로 산책을 시켜 줄 것이고 가끔 공원에 데려가서 다른 강아지들과 놀게 해 줄 거예요."

Jenny의 아빠가 말했습니다. "좋은 생각이구나. 주말에는 Mia와 함께 해변이나 하이킹을 갈 수도 있지."

Jenny가 기쁘게 말했습니다. "너무 신나요! 언젠가는 Mia도 저처럼 수영을 잘 하게 되었으면 좋겠어요! 우리가 같이 하이킹할 때, Mia가 아름다운 풍경을 보면 어떤 기분일지도 궁금해요."

가족이 주차장에 도착했을 때 Jenny는 마음속으로 다짐했습니다. Jenny는 Mia가 가족과 함께 행복한 삶을 살 수 있도록 최선을 다해 돌보겠다고 약속했습니다.

26. 이 이야기는 무엇에 관한 것입니까?

(A) 산으로 떠나는 여행
(B) 강아지에 대한 영상
(C) 새로운 가족 구성원

27. Jenny가 Mia를 어떻게 돌보나요?

(A) 음식을 만들어 주기
(B) 오래 산책 시키기
(C) 해외여행에 데려가기

해설 Jenny는 새로 입양할 강아지 Mia에게 하루 두 번 이상 밥을 주고, 긴 산책을 시켜주며, 공원에서의 교류, 주말에는 바다나 산에도 데려간다고 했다. 하지만 직접 음식을 만든다는 말은 없었고, 해외에 데려간다는 내용도 없어 정답은 (B)이다.

28. Jenny는 평일에 Mia를 어디로 데려갈 것입니까?

(A) 공원
(B) 해변
(C) 산

29. Jenny의 엄마가 Jenny를 대단하다고 생각한 이유는 무엇인가요?

(A) 물을 많이 마셔서
(B) 개들이 물을 많이 마셔야 한다는 사실을 알아서
(C) Mia가 물을 많이 마시고 싶어 한다는 것을 알아서

[30-33] 다음을 읽고, 30-33번 질문에 답하세요.

Tommy와 Tommy의 엄마가 동네 식료품점에서 이번 주 식료품 쇼핑 목록을 확인하고 있습니다. Tommy의 엄마는 Tommy가 쇼핑 목록을 보며 찡그리고 있는 것을 알아채고 Tommy에게 균형 잡힌 식사의 중요성을 이야기해 주기로 마음 먹습니다.

Tommy의 엄마가 말했습니다. "Tommy, 게임 하나 할까. 엄마가 필요

한 물건을 설명하면, 네가 맞춰봐!"

기분이 훨씬 나아진 Tommy는 "재밌을 것 같아. 첫 번째 질문은 뭐야" 라고 답했습니다.

엄마는 "뼈와 이가 튼튼해지려면 이것이 필요해. 보통 흰색이고, 차고 신선하게 보관하기 위해 냉장고에 넣어 두지."라고 설명합니다.

Tommy가 웃으며 대답합니다. "나 정답 알아. 우유잖아! 엄마가 매일 한 컵씩 마시라고 하는 것."

엄마는 "맞았어! 그럼, 다음 질문. 이건 크기가 작고, 색깔과 모양이 다양해. 샐러드, 파스타에 넣고, 스튜에도 들어가. 이건 뭘까?"라고 질문했습니다.

Tommy의 머릿속에 검고 흰 조약돌이 떠올랐습니다 "콩! 콩은 단백질이 많이 들어있는데, 단백질은 에너지를 만들고 튼튼한 근육을 만들어 줘."

엄마는 "맞았어! 이제 마지막 문제 준비됐니? 힌트를 줄게. 이건 네가 좋아하는 채소야. 둥글고 작으며 갈색 껍질이 있어. 보통 껍질을 벗겨서 요리해."라고 물었습니다.

Tommy는 "알아. 감자지? 감자는 여러 맛있는 음식을 만들 수 있어서 좋아. 섬유질도 들어 있어서 소화도 잘 되고, 잠까지 잘 오게 해"라고 답했습니다.

재미있는 시간을 보낸 Tommy는 건강하게 먹는 것이 즐거울 수 있다는 것을 깨달았습니다.

30. 이 대화의 장소는 어디입니까?

(A) 백화점
(B) 창고
(C) 슈퍼마켓

31. 이 이야기는 무엇에 관한 것입니까?

(A) 저녁 식사 재료 구하기
(B) 장보기의 중요성
(C) 건강하게 먹는 것이 즐거울 수 있다는 것을 배우기

32. Tommy의 엄마가 Tommy에게 매일 우유를 마시라고 하는 이유는 무엇입니까?

(A) 우유가 Tommy의 가장 좋아하는 음료여서
(B) Tommy가 튼튼한 뼈를 가지는데 도움이 될 수 있기 때문에
(C) 우유가 항상 냉장고에 들어 있기 때문에

33. 이 게임에서 질문의 답이 <u>아닌</u> 것은 무엇입니까?

(A) 콩
(B) 감자
(C) 소시지

[34-35] 다음을 읽고, 34-35번 질문에 답하세요.

여러 나라에서 온 많은 사람들이 국제우주정거장(ISS)을 건설했습니다. 우주비행사들은 ISS에 머물며 일하고 우주를 탐사합니다. 우주비행사들은 여러 나라 출신으로, 보통 영어와 러시아어로 소통합니다. 그들은 모두 팀으로 일하는데, 이 팀을 크루라고 합니다. 국제우주정

거장은 매우 커서, 실제로 길이가 축구장만큼 깁니다. 우주비행사들은 우주에 대해 더 많이 알기 위해 많은 실험을 합니다. 그들은 자신들이 알아낸 것을 이메일이나 전화로 사람들에게 알려주는데, 이는 마치 집에서 전화를 사용하는 것과 비슷합니다. 우주비행사들이 청결을 유지할 수 있도록 물을 재활용하는 특수 기계도 있습니다. ISS에는 중력이 거의 없기 때문에 우주비행사들은 지구에서와는 다르게 행동해야 합니다. 그들은 공중에 떠다니면서 손과 발로 벽을 밀면서 이동합니다.

34. 사람들은 왜 국제우주정거장을 만들었습니까?

(A) 로켓을 만들고 싶어서
(B) 우주에 대해 더 많이 알고 싶어서
(C) 축구장을 만들고 싶어서

35. 우주비행사들은 왜 손과 발로 벽을 밀어냅니까?

(A) 중력이 거의 없어서
(B) 공기가 없어서
(C) 공간이 거의 없어서

[36-37] 다음을 읽고, 36-37번 질문에 답하세요.

겨울잠(동면)은 특정 동물들이 추운 겨울 동안 오랫동안 잠을 자며 지내는 것을 말합니다. 이 동물들은 먹이가 부족하고 날씨가 추운 겨울을 살아남기 위해 겨울잠을 잡니다. 겨울잠에 들어가기 전에 동물들은 지방을 저장하기 위해 많은 음식을 먹습니다. 겨울잠에 들기 전, 일부 동물들은 생존을 위해 많은 음식을 먹어 몸무게를 평소의 두 배까지 늘릴 수 있습니다. 이 동물들은 또한 잠잘 곳을 찾아야 합니다. 보통 따뜻한 곳에서 안전하게 머물 수 있도록 따뜻하고 어두운 굴 같은 은신처로 이동합니다. 겨울잠에 들어가면 체온이 상당히 떨어지고 호흡 속도도 느려집니다. 많은 동물들이 10월에서 11월 사이에 깊은 겨울잠에 들어가고, 3월에서 4월 사이에 깨어납니다. 여름잠은 완전히 반대입니다. 여름잠은 특정 동물들이 여름에 오랫동안 잠을 자는 것을 말합니다. 이 동물들은 극심한 더위를 이겨내기 위해 여름잠을 자는데, 극심한 더위도 추운 겨울만큼이나 위험할 수 있기 때문입니다. 여름잠을 자면 사냥할 필요가 없어져, 에너지를 절약하고 뜨거운 햇볕을 피하는 데 도움이 됩니다.

36. 겨울잠을 자기 전에 동물들이 많은 음식을 먹는 이유는 무엇입니까?

(A) 잠을 자는 데 모든 에너지를 소모했기 때문에
(B) 살아남으려면 지방을 저장해야 하기 때문에
(C) 다른 동물들과 음식을 나눠 먹기 때문에

해설 동물들이 동면 전에 많은 음식을 먹고 지방을 축적한다는 점이 언급되었고, 일부 동물은 몸무게가 두 배 이상 늘어난다는 내용에 기반하며, 이러한 행동이 생존을 위한 전략임을 고려할 때, 답은 (B)이다.

37. 겨울잠과 여름잠의 차이는 무엇입니까?

(A) 낮에 자는 것과 밤에 자는 것
(B) 육지에서 자는 것과 물에서 자는 것
(C) 추운 계절에 자는 것과 더운 계절에 자는 것

해설 Hibernation과 Estivation은 서로 반대 개념으로 볼 수 있다. Hibernation은 쉽게 말해 동면, 즉 겨울잠이고, Estivation은 여름잠이다. 날씨가 너무 더워서 생존을 위해 일부 동물들이 여름에 긴 잠을 잔다고 언급되어 있으므로, 답은 (C)이다.

Listening

1 (B)	2 (C)	3 (B)	4 (C)
5 (B)	6 (C)	7 (B)	8 (B)
9 (C)	10 (C)	11 (B)	12 (C)
13 (B)	14 (C)	15 (C)	16 (B)
17 (B)	18 (B)	19 (B)	20 (C)
21 (C)	22 (B)	23 (B)	24 (C)
25 (C)	26 (A)	27 (B)	28 (B)
29 (A)	30 (C)	31 (B)	32 (B)
33 (A)	34 (B)	35 (A)	36 (C)
37 (C)	38 (A)	39 (A)	

Part 1.

1.
W: Listen to a mother.
W: Julie, can you help your brother pack his bag? He's having trouble finding his things for school.
W: What did the mother tell her daughter to do?

W: 엄마가 하는 얘기를 들어보세요.
W: Julie, 동생 가방 싸는 것 좀 도와줄래? 동생이 학교에 가지고 갈 준비물을 찾는데 어려움을 겪고 있구나.
W: 엄마는 딸에게 무엇을 하라고 말했습니까?

2.
W: Listen to a gym teacher.
M: I am so proud that we made it to the finals. Now, before our last game tomorrow, I want you all to get a good night's sleep. Keeping in good condition is very important.
W: What did the teacher tell his students to do?

W: 체육 선생님이 하는 얘기를 들어보세요.
M: 우리가 결승전에 진출해서 자랑스럽습니다. 자, 내일 마지막 경기를 앞두고 모두 푹 자도록 하세요. 좋은 컨디션을 유지하는 것이 매우 중요합니다.
W: 선생님은 학생들에게 무엇을 하라고 말했습니까?

3.

W: Listen to a mother.

W: Jenna, are you ready to go? Before going to dinner, we have to pick up your brother from soccer practice, and we're running late. Your dad will be picking up your sister from ballet class.

W: What did the mother ask her daughter to do?

W: 엄마가 하는 얘기를 들어보세요.

W: Jenna, 갈 준비됐어? 저녁 먹으러 가기 전에 오빠를 축구 연습장에서 픽업해야 하는데, 우리 지금 늦었어. 여동생은 아빠가 발레 수업에서 픽업할 거야.

W: 엄마는 딸에게 무엇을 하라고 요청했습니까?

4.

W: Listen to a girl.

G: Do you remember telling me about the new mall that was built? It's huge! It's the biggest one I've ever seen. There's a large cinema and even an ice rink. We didn't have time yesterday, so my sister and I couldn't go ice skating. I know how much you wanted to check it out! How about we go together?

W: What did the girl ask her friend to do?

W: 소녀가 하는 얘기를 들어보세요.

G: 너 나한테 새로 생긴 쇼핑몰에 대해 이야기했던 것 기억나? 정말 크더라! 내가 본 것 중에 가장 큰 쇼핑몰이야. 큰 영화관도 있고 심지어 아이스링크도 있어. 어제는 시간이 없어서 언니랑 나는 아이스 스케이트를 못 탔어. 너 정말 가고 싶어 했잖아. 우리 같이 가볼까?

W: 소녀는 친구에게 무엇을 하자고 요청했습니까?

5.

W: Listen to a father.

M: If you guess what this word is, Jenny, we'll buy one this afternoon. Are you ready? It's usually a thick book filled with all kinds of words. In fact, there is one for every language in the world. There is even your favorite word in it: mangoes!

W: What did the father tell his daughter to do?

W: 아빠가 하는 얘기를 들어보세요.

M: Jenny, 이 단어가 무엇인지 맞히면 오늘 오후에 그걸 사 줄게. 준비됐어? 이건 보통 두꺼운 책이고, 온갖 단어가 가득 들어 있어. 세상의 모든 언어마다 이런 책이 하나씩 있지. 네가 가장 좋아하는 단어인 '망고'도 들어 있어.

W: 아빠는 딸에게 무엇을 하라고 말했습니까?

6.

W: Listen to a teacher.

M: Hold out your arm and clench your fist. The size of your heart is about the size of your fist. The heart acts as a pump, sending blood throughout our bodies. Inside the blood is oxygen from your lungs; our bodies need oxygen-rich blood to stay alive and healthy. We will focus today on the connection between our lungs and our heart. However, I first want you to turn to page 7 and start reading about it.

W: What did the teacher tell his students to do?

W: 선생님이 하는 얘기를 들어보세요.

M: 팔을 뻗고 주먹을 쥐어 보세요. 우리 심장의 크기는 주먹 정도의 크기입니다. 심장은 펌프와 같이 우리 몸 전체에 피를 보냅니다. 그 피 안에는 폐에서 온 산소가 들어 있는데, 우리 몸은 살아 있고 건강하기 위해서는 산소가 풍부한 피가 필요합니다. 오늘은 폐와 심장의 연결에 대해 집중해 볼 거예요. 그 전에, 7쪽을 펴서 읽어 보세요.

W: 선생님은 학생들에게 무엇을 하라고 했습니까?

7.

W: Listen to a music teacher.

W: I know that practice can be hard, but putting in your efforts will bring great results. Amanda, how about we try again? Pick up your bow and try to rest your cello against your chest. That's right; now, use your right hand to hold the bow and your left hand to press down the strings. This will help you make beautiful sounds.

W: What did the teacher tell her student to do?

W: 음악 선생님이 하는 얘기를 들어보세요.

W: 연습이 어렵다는 것은 알지만, 열심히 노력하면 좋은 결과가 있을 거야. Amanda, 우리 다시 해볼까? 활을 들어 첼로를 가슴에 기대 보렴. 좋아, 이제 오른손으로 활을 잡고 왼손으로 줄을 눌러보자. 이렇게 하면 아름다운 소리를 낼 수 있을 거야.

W: 선생님은 학생에게 무엇을 하라고 말했습니까?

8.

W: Listen to a father.

M: How about we go and wash the car? It's a great day, and the car needs cleaning. You can help me wash it from top to bottom, and we can even have fun polishing it. Afterward, why don't we order pizza? I know that pepperoni is your favorite.

W: What did the father ask his daughter to do?

W: 아빠가 하는 얘기를 들어보세요.

M: 우리 차를 세차하러 가는게 어때? 차도 세차가 필요해보여. 네가 윗부분부터 아랫부분까지 세차하는 걸 도와주렴. 광내는 것도 재미있을 거야. 다 마치면 피자 먹자. 페퍼로니 제일 좋아하잖아.

W: 아빠는 딸에게 무엇을 하자고 요청했나요?

Part 2.

9.

M: Listen to a conversation between a boy and girl. Listen for the answer to this question.

B: Will Mom let me go to the baseball game tonight?

G: Have you finished your science project?

B: No, not yet; it seems to take forever.

G: I don't think she's going to let you go unless you finish it. It's due next week, right?

B: Yes, I'd better get to it then.

M: What will the boy do next?

M: 소년과 소녀 사이의 대화를 듣고 질문에 답하세요.

B: 엄마가 오늘 밤 야구 경기에 가게 허락하실까?

G: 과학 프로젝트는 다 끝났어?

B: 아직. 끝이 안나는 것 같아.

G: 그거 끝내지 않으면 못 가게 하실걸. 다음 주가 마감이지?

B: 응. 그럼 얼른 해야 겠다.

M: 소년은 다음에 무엇을 할까요?

(A) 야구 경기에 간다.

(B) 엄마에게 야구 경기에 가도 되는지 물어본다.

(C) 다음 주까지 제출해야 하는 프로젝트를 하러 간다.

10.

M: Listen to a conversation between a father and his daughter. Listen for the answer to this question.

M: Are you excited about this weekend?

G: Did we have plans?

M: No, not yet. But the weather will be great, so we could do something.

G: Do you want to go camping? One of my friends went camping last week, and said he had a lot of fun.

M: Well, how about going to the beach or something for cooler air?

G: I wouldn't mind going to the lake near grandma's house.

M: Well, what shall we do then?

G: Why don't we think it over and decide tomorrow morning?

M: What are they talking about?

M: 아빠와 딸 사이의 대화를 듣고 질문에 답하세요.

M: 이번 주말 기대되니?

G: 우리 계획 있어요?

M: 아직 없어. 하지만 날씨가 좋으니 뭔가 할 수 있겠지.

G: 캠핑 가는 것은 어때요? 한 친구가 지난주에 캠핑 갔다 왔는데 정말 재미있었대요.

M: 음... 시원하게 해변 같은 데 가는 건 어떠니?

G: 할머니 집 근처 호수에 가는 것도 괜찮아요.

M: 그러면 그렇게 할까?

G: 내일 아침에 다시 생각해 보고 결정하는 건 어때요?

M: 아빠와 딸은 무엇에 대해 이야기하고 있습니까?

(A) 해변으로 놀러 가기

(B) 산으로 하이킹 가기

(C) 주말 계획

11.

M: Listen to a conversation between a boy and a girl. Listen for the answer to this question.

B: Our winter vacation starts next week! I'm so excited.

G: Me, too! It's only a week away.

B: Do you have any plans for the vacation?

G: No, nothing special. I plan on getting rest. I really need it.

B: That's good. It's important to get rest during the breaks.

G: Right. How about you? Do you have any plans?

B: Yes, I'm going to visit my grandmother and go skiing with my family. She lives in Canada. Canada's winter is perfect for skiing.

G: That sounds like a lot of fun. Please take me next time. I love skiing.

M: Which is NOT true about the boy?

M: 소년과 소녀 사이의 대화를 듣고 질문에 답하세요.

B: 다음 주면 겨울방학 시작이야. 정말 기대돼.

G: 나도! 일주일밖에 안 남았어.

B: 방학 동안 계획 있어?

G: 아니, 특별한 계획 없어. 푹 쉴 생각이야. 휴식이 필요해.

B: 좋은 생각이야. 방학 때 쉬는 건 정말 중요해.

G: 맞아. 너는? 계획 있어?

B: 응, 가족이랑 할머니 집에 가서 스키 탈 거야. 할머니가 캐나다에 사시거든. 캐나다 겨울은 스키 타기 딱 이야.

G: 진짜 재미있겠다. 다음엔 나도 데려가 줘. 나 스키 타는 걸 정말 좋아하거든.

M: 소년에 대한 설명으로 옳지 않은 것은 무엇입니까?

(A) 겨울방학을 기대하고 있다.

(B) 방학 동안 특별한 계획이 없다.

(C) 할머니 집을 방문할 예정이다.

12.

M: Listen to a conversation between a father and his son. Listen for the answer to this question.

B: Dad, I finally did a backhand using only one hand.

M: Great job, Sisco! Now, how about we practice a serve?

B: It's so hard to get the ball over the net.

M: All you need is a little practice. Try to hit the ball when it is at its highest point.

B: Like this?

M: Excellent job; I knew you could do it.

B: Thanks, Dad. Can we come and practice every weekend? I love spending time with you.

M: Sounds like a plan.

M: Why does the boy want to practice again tomorrow?

M: 아빠와 아들 사이의 대화를 듣고 질문에 답하세요.

B: 아빠, 드디어 한 손으로 백핸드를 성공했어요!
M: 잘했구나, Sisco! 이제 서브 연습을 해보는 건 어때?
B: 공을 네트 너머로 넘기는 게 너무 어려워요.
M: 약간의 연습만 하면 돼. 공이 가장 높이 올라갔을 때 쳐봐.
B: 이렇게요?
M: 아주 잘했어! 할 수 있을 줄 알았어.
B: 고마워요, 아빠. 매주 주말마다 와서 연습할 수 있을까요? 아빠
랑 함께하는 시간이 정말 좋아요.
M: 좋은 생각이다.

M: 아들은 왜 내일 다시 연습하고 싶어 하나요?

(A) 백핸드 연습을 하고 싶어서
(B) 서브를 잘 하고 싶어서
(C) 아빠와 시간을 보내는 것이 좋아서

13.
M: Listen to a conversation between two students at school.
Listen for the answer to this question.

G: Did you hear that Daisy has returned from her trip to
France?
B: Not only did I hear it, but I saw her yesterday.
G: Lucky you! Did she tell you about her trip?
B: I couldn't ask her. I had to go to basketball practice.
G: That's too bad. My family is going to France this summer,
and I want to know everything she did.
B: You're going to France? I thought you were going to
Spain.
G: I'm going to both, but we're stopping in Spain first and
then going to France.
B: Sounds awesome! Why not give her a call?
G: I was just about to!

M: What does the girl want to do?

M: 학교에서 두 학생 사이의 대화를 듣고 질문에 답하세요.

G: Daisy가 프랑스 여행에서 돌아온 거 들었어?
B: 들었지. 어제 Daisy를 보기도 했는걸.
G: 좋겠다. 여행 얘기 들었어?
B: 못 물어봤어. 농구 연습 가야 했거든.
G: 아쉽다. 우리 가족이 이번 여름에 프랑스 갈 거라서 Daisy가 뭐
했는지 다 알고 싶어.
B: 프랑스에 간다고? 난 너 스페인 가는 줄 알았는데.
G: 두 나라 모두 가. 먼저 스페인에 들렀다가 프랑스로 갈 거야.
B: 끝내주는데! Daisy에게 전화해 봐.
G: 막 전화하려던 참이었어.

M: 소녀가 하고 싶어 하는 것은 무엇인가요?

(A) 프랑스에서 Daisy 만나기
(B) Daisy로부터 스페인 여행에 대해 듣기
(C) Daisy에게 전화해 여행이 어땠는지 묻기

14.
M: Listen to a conversation between a receptionist and a
guest. Listen for the answer to this question.

W: Good morning. Thank you for calling West Life Hotel.
How may I help you today?
M: Hi, I would like to make a reservation for next weekend.
W: Sure, how many rooms do you need?
M: I would like two rooms, please.
W: OK, we have a family room and a double. Which ones
would you like?
M: How many beds are in each room?
W: There is a king bed and a single bed for the family room,
and two single beds for the double.
M: I'll take two family rooms, please.
W: No problem. Is there anything else I can assist you with?
M: No, that will be all. Thank you.

M: What did the front desk ask the man?

M: 다음 직원과 고객 사이의 대화를 듣고 질문에 답하세요.

W: 안녕하세요. 웨스트 라이프 호텔에 전화 주셔서 감사합니다. 무
엇을 도와 드릴까요?
M: 안녕하세요. 다음 주말을 예약하고 싶습니다.
W: 몇 개의 객실이 필요하신가요?
M: 두 개 필요합니다.
W: 알겠습니다. 패밀리룸과 더블룸이 있는데, 어떤 것을 예약하시
겠습니까?
M: 각 방에 침대가 몇 개 있나요?
W: 패밀리룸에는 킹사이즈 침대 하나와 싱글 사이즈 침대가 하나
있고, 더블룸에는 싱글 사이즈 침대가 두 개 있습니다.
M: 그럼 패밀리룸 두 개로 하겠습니다.
W: 알겠습니다. 다른 도와드릴 사항이 있을까요?
M: 없습니다. 이걸로 충분합니다. 감사합니다.

M: 직원이 남자에게 물어본 것은 무엇입니까?

(A) 체크인할 인원수
(B) 남자의 개인정보
(C) 예약하고자 하는 객실의 수

15.
M: Listen to a conversation between two students. Listen
for the answer to this question.

G: Why do you look so nervous?
B: I usually remember all my lines, but my mind goes blank
whenever I'm on stage.

G: It's because you feel anxious. Don't worry; I'm sure many people feel the same way you do.

B: Are you sure?

G: Absolutely, but if you're worried, how about we go and ask Mrs. Thatcher if we can practice on the school stage?

B: Do you think she'll agree? That would help.

G: Sure, why not go and ask her now? The stage is probably free now.

M: Why is the boy feeling nervous?

M: 두 학생 사이의 대화를 듣고 질문에 답하세요.

G: 왜 그렇게 긴장하고 있어?

B: 항상 대사를 다 외우는데도 무대에만 올라가면 머릿속이 하얘져.

G: 불안해하니까 그런 거야. 걱정하지 마. 다른 사람들도 너처럼 느껴.

B: 정말?

G: 당연하지. 그래도 걱정되면 Thatcher 선생님께 가서 학교 무대에서 연습해도 되는지 여쭤보는 건 어때?

B: 선생님이 허락하실까? 그렇게 할 수 있으면 좋을 텐데.

G: 물론이지. 지금 가서 여쭤보자. 학교 무대가 항상 사용되고 있는 것은 아니니까.

M: 소년이 긴장한 이유는 무엇입니까?

(A) 대사를 외우는데 어려움을 겪는다.
(B) Thatcher 선생님의 수업을 제대로 준비하지 못했다.
(C) 무대에 올라가면 얼어붙는다.

16.

M: Listen to a conversation between a father and his daughter. Listen for the answer to this question.

G: Dad, I think I left my science project in the car.

M: I'm on my way to the car right now. Do you know where you put it?

G: If I remember correctly, I put it in the front seat.

M: Ah ha! It's here, do you need it today?

G: Yes, I have to hand it in to my science teacher. The science fair is next week.

M: OK, I'll drop it off. Can you meet me outside of school in half an hour?

G: Yes, thanks, Dad.

M: Why does the girl need her science project?

M: 아빠와 딸 사이의 대화를 듣고 질문에 답하세요.

G: 아빠, 과학 프로젝트 한 걸 차에 두고 온 것 같아요.

M: 지금 마침 차로 가고 있어. 어디에 뒀는지 기억나?

G: 기억이 맞다면 앞좌석에 뒀을 거예요.

M: 앗, 여기 있네. 오늘 필요해?

G: 네. 과학 선생님께 제출해야 해요. 다음 주 과학 전시회가 있거든요.

M: 알았어. 갖다줄게. 학교 밖에서 30분 후에 만나.

G: 감사해요, 아빠.

M: 딸은 왜 과학 프로젝트 결과물이 필요한가요?

(A) 친구에게 보여주려고
(B) 선생님께 제출해야 해서
(C) 오늘 열리는 과학 전시회를 위해

Part 3.

17.

G: Hi, this is Jenny. I had a great time at dinner last night, so I wanted to tell you how much I appreciated it. It was the first time I've been to a Greek restaurant. My favorite part of the dinner was the delicious salad. How about you come to my house for dinner tonight? Call me back!

M: Why did Jenny call?

G: 안녕, 나 Jenny야. 어젯밤 저녁 정말 즐거웠고, 너무 고맙다는 말을 하고 싶었어. 그리스 음식점을 가본 것은 처음이었어. 식사 중에 가장 좋았던 것은 정말 맛있는 샐러드였어. 오늘 저녁은 우리 집에 와서 함께하는 거 어때? 전화 부탁해.

M: Jenny는 왜 전화했나요?

(A) 일식 레스토랑을 추천하려고
(B) 어젯밤 저녁 식사에 대한 감사를 전하려고
(C) 맛있는 그리스 레스토랑에 대해 물어보려고

18.

W: Attention, please! The school is having an essay contest. The topic is "Ways to improve school life." The winners will be awarded the top prize. English teachers will judge the essays. The deadline to turn in the essays is next Tuesday. The winners will be announced next Friday. Good luck, everyone!

M: Which of the following is true about the essay contest?

W: 여러분, 주목하세요. 본교에서 에세이 대회를 개최합니다. 주제는 '학교생활을 개선하는 법'입니다. 우승자에게는 최고의 상이 수여됩니다. 영어 선생님들이 에세이를 심사할 예정입니다. 에세이 제출 마감일은 다음 주 화요일입니다. 수상자는 다음 주 금요일에 발표됩니다. 모두 좋은 결과 있길 바랍니다!

M: 다음 중 에세이 대회에 대한 사실로 옳은 것은 무엇인가요?

(A) 학생들이 어떤 주제든지 선택할 수 있다.
(B) 영어 선생님들이 에세이를 심사한다.
(C) 마감일은 이번 주 금요일이다.

19.

M: Good afternoon, Mrs. Thompson. The television you ordered has just arrived at our store. Would you like it delivered, or will you be picking it up? If you need it delivered, should I send it to the address you gave? If you plan to come by the store, please let me know, since we will be closing an hour earlier today.

M: Why did the store employee call?

M: 안녕하세요, Thompson 부인. 주문하신 텔레비전이 방금 저희 매장에 도착했습니다. 배송을 원하시나요, 아니면 직접 오셔서 가져가시겠습니까? 배송을 원하신다면 이전에 주신 주소로 보내 드리면 될까요? 오늘은 매장이 한 시간 일찍 문을 닫기 때문에 직접 오실 예정이라면 말씀해 주세요.

M: 매장 직원은 왜 전화를 했습니까?

(A) Thompson 부인에게 주소를 물어보기 위해
(B) Thompson 부인에게 구매한 물건이 도착했음을 알리기 위해
(C) 텔레비전을 집으로 보냈다고 알리기 위해

20.

B: Hi, Grandma, it's Daniel. I hope you're having a great day! I'm at your house and noticed you are not home, but I wanted to ask you for a quick favor. We have an important presentation at school today about our family, and the family photo album would be really helpful. I remember all the wonderful pictures of our family enjoying special moments together. Can you tell me where I can find it? I promise to take great care of it and return it immediately after school tomorrow.

M: What will Daniel do tomorrow?

B: 할머니, 안녕하세요. Daniel이예요. 잘 지내고 계시죠? 저 지금 할머니 댁에 왔는데, 안 계신 것 같아요. 부탁을 하나 드리려고요. 오늘 학교에서 가족에 대한 발표가 있는데, 가족사진 앨범이 있으면 좋을 것 같아요. 우리 가족이 특별한 순간들을 함께한 멋진 사진들이 생각나서요. 그 앨범이 어디 있는지 알려주실 수 있나요? 조심해서 쓰고 내일 학교 끝나면 바로 돌려드릴게요.

M: Daniel은 내일 무엇을 할 예정입니까?

(A) 가족 앨범에 사진을 추가한다.
(B) 학교에서 가족에 대한 발표를 한다.
(C) 가족사진 앨범을 돌려준다.

21.

M: Hello, Diane, it's Mr. Chancelor. As you know, we're having a fundraising sale soon. All the students have brought a lot of goods from their homes. I was amazed to see the stock all piled up. One student even brought signed books of famous authors! I'm calling because I have a favor to ask. Could you make a poster for this event? The money we raise will go somewhere meaningful, and it would be wonderful if you could contribute your artistic talent. Please let me know soon.

M: Why did Mr. Chancelor call Diane?

M: 안녕, Diane, Chancelor 선생님이야. 알다시피 곧 모금 행사가 있어. 모든 학생이 집에서 다양한 물품을 가져 왔어. 쌓여 있는 물건들을 보고 놀랐단다. 어떤 학생은 유명 작가가 서명한 책까지 가져왔더라고. 내가 Diane 너에게 전화한 이유는 부탁할 일이 있어서야. 이 행사에 사용할 포스터를 한 장 만들어 줄 수 있을까? 우리가 모은 돈은 의미 있는 곳에 쓰일 예정이라서, 혹시 너의 예술적 재능을 기부해줄 수 있다면 고마울 것 같아. 곧 알려줘.

M: Chancelor씨는 왜 Diane에게 전화했나요?

(A) 모금 행사에 대한 계획을 세우기 위해
(B) 서명된 책을 가져온 것에 대해 감사하기 위해
(C) 행사에 사용할 포스터를 만들어 줄 수 있는지 물어보기 위해

Part 4.

[22-25] 다음을 듣고, 22-25번 질문에 답하세요.

M: "Has the plane arrived yet?" asked Kate, bouncing on her toes excitedly. She had been standing in the airport arrival hall for half an hour, holding a bouquet in one hand and a sign with Yuha's name in the other. "I don't think it will be long now, Kate. The arrival board says the plane has landed. I think Yuha is getting her luggage," replied her mom. Kate and Yuha had been pen pals for over three years, and this was their first meeting in person. With the Easter holidays approaching, Kate had invited Yuha to England for a visit.
"Mom, how about seeing Big Ben and the Tower of London tomorrow? Then we can visit Buckingham Palace, and maybe even go on the Harry Potter Studio Tour! Yuha mentioned in her letters that she wants to see those places, especially the Palace," Kate suggested. Knowing how much Kate wanted to show Yuha all the places they had talked about in their letters, her mom looked at her lovingly and said, "You are such a good friend, Kate. I love how you have everything planned out for Yuha."
"Thanks, Mom! Do you think there's anything Yuha can't eat? She didn't mention it in her letters, but we should ask her again to be sure. Oh, I nearly forgot! Mom, do you think it's OK if we go to Grandma's house this weekend? One of the things Yuha and I have in common is our love for baking. She mentioned wanting to make an apple crumble, and you know Grandma's pies are amazing! Maybe she can teach us how to make one," Kate continued.

M: "비행기 도착했어요?" Kate가 들썩이며 들뜬 목소리로 물었다. Kate는 공항 입국장에서 한 손에는 꽃다발을, 다른 손에는 Yuha의 이름이 적힌 팻말을 들고 30분 동안 서 있었다. 엄마가 "이제 곧 도

착할 것 같아. 도착 전광판에 비행기가 착륙했다고 뜨네. 아마 Yuha가 짐을 찾고 있는 것 같아."라고 대답했다. Kate와 Yuha는 3년이 넘는 펜팔 친구다. 이번은 그들이 처음으로 직접 만나는 순간이다. 부활절 연휴가 다가오자, Kate가 Yuha를 영국으로 초대한 것이다.

"엄마, 내일 Big Ben이랑 Tower of London 보러 가는 건 어때요? 그 다음엔 Buckingham Palace도 보고, 가능하면 Harry Potter Studio 투어도 가면 좋겠어요. Yuha가 편지에서 가고 싶다고 한 곳들이거든요, 특히 Buckingham Palace이요." Kate가 제안했다. 엄마는 Kate가 Yuha에게 편지로 나눈 이야기 속 장소들을 보여주고 싶어 하는 마음을 알고는 Kate를 사랑스럽게 바라보며 말했다. "넌 정말 좋은 친구구나, Kate. Yuha를 위해 이렇게 계획을 세웠다니 기특하다."

"고마워요, 엄마. Yuha가 못 먹는 음식이 있을까요? 편지에서 언급한 적은 없지만, 다시 한번 확인해 보는 게 좋겠어요. 아참, 깜빡할 뻔했어요. 엄마, 이번 주말에 할머니 집에 가도 될까요? Yuha랑 제가 둘 다 너무 좋아하는 게 베이킹이잖아요. Yuha가 사과 크럼블을 만들고 싶다고 했는데, 할머니가 만든 파이가 최고잖아요. 할머니가 파이 만드는 법을 알려주실 수 있지 않을까요?" Kate가 말을 이었다.

22. Kate가 신이 난 이유는 무엇입니까?

(A) 공항에 처음 가보기 때문에
(B) 펜팔 친구를 기다리고 있기 때문에
(C) 비행기를 타는 것이 기대돼서

23. Yuha가 가장 방문하고 싶어 하는 곳은 어디입니까?

(A) Tower of London
(B) Buckingham Palace
(C) Harry Potter Studio

24. Kate가 Yuha에게 무엇을 물어보려고 합니까?

(A) 짐을 찾는 데 도움이 필요한지
(B) 부활절 연휴 동안 방문하고 싶은지
(C) 어떤 음식을 피해야 하는지

25. Kate가 할머니 집에 가고 싶어 하는 이유는 무엇입니까?

(A) Yuha가 할머니의 음식을 먹어보게 하고 싶어서
(B) 할머니 댁의 사과를 쓰고 싶어서
(C) 할머니로부터 사과 크럼블 만드는 법을 배우고 싶어서

[26-29] 다음을 듣고, 26-29번 질문에 답하세요.

> W: "Mom, I don't know if I can do this. Can you see how sweaty my palms are? After my last speech competition, it's so hard for me to speak in front of so many people," said Shelby in a worried voice. Shelby and her parents were in the car on their way to her musical performance. Although she usually felt confident on stage, she had lost much of her self-assurance after forgetting her lines at the last speech competition. To her, it felt like a hurdle she couldn't overcome.
>
> "Shelby, everyone makes mistakes. Don't be too hard on yourself. Nobody noticed. Not even I realized that you had forgotten your lines," her dad said reassuringly. "That's right, Shelby. No one is perfect. Besides, mistakes are part of learning. Forgetting your lines once isn't a big deal, I promise," her mom encouraged. Shelby usually felt comfortable on-stage during presentations, speeches, and performances because she practiced hard and did her best each time.
>
> "We still have plenty of time before the performance. How about we stop by the park and practice one more time? I think it will help you to recite your lines again in an open space. Plus, a good walk can help calm your nerves," her dad suggested. Hearing their reassuring words, Shelby felt a renewed sense of determination. It was as if a voice inside her said, "Everyone slips up sometimes; let's take the plunge!"

W: "엄마, 나 이거 할 수 있을지 모르겠어. 내 손바닥에 땀 나는 것 좀 봐. 지난번 말하기 대회 이후로 많은 사람들 앞에서 말하는 게 너무 힘들어." Shelby가 걱정 가득한 목소리로 말했다. Shelby와 Shelby의 부모는 차를 타고 Shelby의 뮤지컬 공연장으로 가는 중이었다. Shelby는 무대에서 자신 있어 하는 편이었지만, 지난번 말하기 대회에서 대사를 잊어버린 후로 자신감을 많이 잃은 상태였다. Shelby는 극복할 수 없는 걸림돌이 있는 것처럼 느꼈다.

"Shelby, 누구나 실수를 해. 너무 자책하지 마. 아무도 눈치채지 못했고, 나도 네가 대사를 잊은 줄도 몰랐어." Shelby의 아빠가 안심시키며 말했다.

"맞아, Shelby. 완벽한 사람은 없어. 그리고 실수는 배움의 일부야. 한 번 대사를 잊은 건 별일 아니야, 정말이야." 엄마가 격려했다. Shelby는 매번 열심히 연습하고 최선을 다했기 때문에 평소에는 발표, 연설, 공연에서 무대에 서는 것을 편하게 느꼈다.

"아직 공연 전까지 시간이 많아. 공원에 들러서 한 번 더 연습해 볼까? 야외에서 대사를 다시 읊어보면 도움이 될 거야. 가볍게 걸으면서 긴장도 풀고." 아빠가 제안했다. 부모님의 안심시키는 말을 들으며 Shelby는 새로운 결심을 다졌다. 마치 그녀 안의 목소리가 말하는 것 같았다. "누구나 가끔 실수를 해. 과감히 도전해 보자!"

26. 이 이야기는 무엇에 관한 것입니까?

(A) Shelby가 어떻게 두려움을 극복하는지
(B) Shelby가 어떻게 두려움을 계속 붙잡고 있는지
(C) Shelby가 어떻게 말하기 대회를 앞두고 긴장하고 있는지

해설 Shelby가 발표나 스피치에서 항상 잘하는 이유는 늘 최선을 다하기 때문이며, 지난 스피치 대회 때 대사를 잊었던 경험이 있어서 이번 음악 공연에서는 긴장되는 마음이 더 크게 느껴진다. 하지만 부모님의

응원과 자신의 노력을 스스로 알고 있기에 두려움을 극복하는 내용으로, 정답은 (A)이다.

27. Shelby가 자신감을 잃은 이유는 무엇입니까?

(A) 다른 사람들이 훨씬 잘해서
(B) 대회에 사람들이 너무 많아서
(C) 무대에 섰을 때 머릿속이 하얘져서

28. Shelby의 부모님이 하지 <u>않은</u> 말은 무엇입니까?

(A) 모든 실수는 발전할 기회다.
(B) 말하기 대회에서 모든 사람이 셀비를 응원했다.
(C) 무언가를 잊어도 큰일이 아니다.

29. Shelby는 다시 어떻게 결심을 다졌습니까?

(A) 용기를 내서 도전해 보기로
(B) 시간을 벌어서 다음 기회를 잡기로
(C) 대사를 더 잘 외우기로

해설 Shelby는 누구나 실수할 수 있다는 점을 받아들였고, 자신이 얼마나 노력해왔는지 알고 있기에 다시 용기를 얻을 수 있었다. 오늘 있을 음악 공연에도 최선을 다하겠다는 의지를 보였다는 점에 기반해, 두려움을 극복하는 내용이라고 볼 수 있다. 따라서 정답은 (A)이다.

[30-33] 다음을 듣고, 30-33번 질문에 답하세요.

M: Each flower is unique in its own way, having different meanings to people and situations. For example, they play a big role in our celebrations, and people often give carnations to show love and gratitude at graduations or give sunflowers to help cheer someone up. Also, most nations have their national flower, each carrying its special meaning. These flowers are important because they show cultural values and history.
The rose, for instance, is the national flower of the United States. With its bright colors and sweet fragrances, it stands for love, beauty, and courage. This is why, when you get a rose from someone, you know how much this person cares for you. Next, in India, the pink lotus that blooms proudly is the national flower. This beautiful flower grows well even in muddy waters but still blooms, symbolizing purity and peace. It reminds people that they can shine brightly no matter how tough things get. Moving to Italy, although Italy does not officially have a national flower, people see the white lily as representing beauty and purity. These elegant flowers remind us that strength can coexist with beauty, even in challenging situations. By appreciating these flowers, we can learn about different cultures and the things that connect us all.

M: 각 꽃은 저마다 고유해서, 사람과 상황에 따라 다른 의미를 지닙니다. 예를 들어, 꽃은 우리의 축하 의식에서 중요한 역할을 합니다. 사람들은 졸업식에서 사랑과 감사를 표현하기 위해 카네이션을 선물하기도 하고, 누군가를 응원하기 위해 해바라기를 주기도 합니다. 또한 대부분의 국가에는 특별한 의미를 담은 국화가 있습니다. 이러한 꽃들은 문화적 가치와 역사를 보여주기 때문에 중요합니다. 예를 들어, 장미는 미국의 국화입니다. 선명한 색과 달콤한 향기를 지닌 장미는 사랑, 아름다움, 용기를 상징합니다. 그래서 누군가에게 장미를 받는다면, 그 사람이 당신을 얼마나 아끼는지 알 수 있습니다. 다음으로 인도에서는 당당하게 피어나는 분홍색 연꽃이 국화입니다. 이 아름다운 꽃은 진흙탕 속에서도 잘 자라고 활짝 피어나며, 순수함과 평화를 상징합니다. 이는 어떤 힘든 상황에서도 밝게 빛날 수 있다는 것을 일깨워줍니다. 이탈리아로 가면, 이탈리아에는 공식적인 국화는 없지만 흔히 하얀 백합이 국화처럼 여겨집니다. 백합은 아름다움과 순수함을 대표합니다. 이 우아한 꽃은 어려운 상황 속에서도 강인함과 아름다움이 함께할 수 있다는 것을 상기시켜 줍니다. 꽃을 감상하고 그 의미를 알아감으로써 우리는 다양한 문화를 배우고, 우리 모두를 연결해주는 공통의 가치를 발견할 수 있습니다.

30. 어떤 국가들에 국화가 있는 이유는 무엇입니까?

(A) 과거에는 모든 국가가 국화를 가져야 했기 때문에
(B) 전 세계 모든 나라에서 꽃이 자라기 때문에
(C) 국화는 한 국가의 문화와 역사를 대표하기 때문에

해설 대부분의 나라들이 국화를 가지고 있다는 내용은 있었지만, 모든 나라가 국화를 갖고 있으며 예전부터 반드시 있어야 했다는 내용은 확인되지 않았다. 반면, 국화를 가진 나라에서는 그것이 문화, 가치, 역사 등을 반영한다고 언급되었고, 이 점에 기반해, 정답은 (C)이다.

31. 다음 중 본문에 언급된 꽃들에 대한 설명으로 옳지 <u>않은</u> 것은 무엇입니까?

(A) 미국의 국화는 장미이다.
(B) 분홍색 연꽃은 진흙탕에서 잘 자라지 못한다.
(C) 사람들은 졸업식에서 카네이션을 자주 선물한다.

32. 다음 중 국화로 언급된 꽃은 무엇입니까?

(A) 카네이션
(B) 분홍색 연꽃
(C) 하얀 백합

33. 이탈리아에 대한 설명으로 옳은 것은 무엇입니까?

(A) 이탈리아는 국화가 없다.
(B) 하얀 백합은 이탈리아의 진흙탕에서 잘 자란다.
(C) 많은 사람이 장미를 이탈리아를 상징하는 꽃으로 여긴다.

W: Wooden pencils have a history of about 2,000 years. Greeks, Romans, and Egyptians used lead pencils, but they were expensive and very poisonous. Then, in the 16th century, a soft black mineral was found clinging to the roots of a fallen tree. It was graphite. It was perfect for writing but was so soft that it needed a holder. The best way discovered was to drill short lengths of wood, hollow them out, and fill them with graphite. Then, people wanted darker or lighter types of pencils. So companies began adding clay to the graphite to make it darker and softer. Letters and numbers were then used to show the darkness or hardness of a pencil. For example, H means Hard, and the hardest pencil made is a 9H. They are very light. HB is medium-dark and means Hard Black. 2B is darker, 3B even darker, and 9B is the darkest you can buy. Pencils are amazing! One pencil can draw a line for 70 kilometers, and it can write under water. So next time you go scuba diving, make sure you have one in your pocket!

W: 나무 연필의 역사는 약 2,000년에 이릅니다. 고대 그리스, 로마, 이집트인들은 납으로 된 연필을 사용했지만, 값 비싸고 매우 독성이 강했습니다. 그러던 중 16세기에 쓰러진 나무의 뿌리에 달라붙은 부드러운 검은색 광물이 발견되었습니다. 바로 흑연이었습니다. 흑연은 글을 쓰기에 완벽했지만 너무 부드러워서 그것을 감쌀 무언가가 필요했습니다. 가장 좋은 방법은 짧은 길이의 나무 조각에 구멍을 뚫고, 속을 비워 그 안에 흑연을 넣는 것이었습니다. 그 후 사람들은 더 진하거나 연한 연필을 원했습니다. 그래서 회사들은 흑연에 점토를 첨가하여 연필심의 단단함과 진하기를 조절했습니다. 이후 연필의 진하기나 단단함을 표시하기 위해 알파벳과 숫자를 사용하게 되었습니다. 예를 들어, H는 'Hard(단단함)'를 의미하는데, 가장 단단한 연필은 9H로 매우 연하게 써집니다. HB는 중간 정도의 진하기로, 'Hard Black(단단한 검정)'을 의미합니다. 2B는 더 진하고, 3B는 그 보다 더 진하며, 9B는 시판되는 연필 중에서 가장 진한 농도의 선을 그립니다.
연필은 놀라운 도구입니다. 연필 한 자루로 70km 길이의 선을 그을 수 있으며, 물속에서도 글씨를 쓸 수 있습니다. 그러니 다음번에 스쿠버다이빙을 갈 때는 주머니에 연필 한 자루를 꼭 챙겨 가세요.

34. 오래전 연필은 어땠습니까?

(A) 저렴하고 사용하기 쉬웠다.
(B) 비싸고 독성이 있었다.
(C) 해롭지는 않았지만 비쌌다.

35. 사람들은 연필에 사용할 나무 조각의 속을 어떻게 비웠습니까?

(A) 나무 조각에 흑연을 채웠다.
(B) 흑연에 점토를 섞었다.
(C) 흑연에 나무를 채웠다.

36. 선생님이 숫자와 글자에 대해 언급한 이유는 무엇입니까?

(A) 연필의 길이를 표시하기 위해
(B) 연필에서 진하기가 얼마나 중요한지 설명하기 위해
(C) 연필의 진하기 정도를 설명하기 위해

[37-39] 다음을 듣고, 37~39번 질문에 답하세요.

M: The universe is immense, and some scientists believe it may even be limitless. Interestingly, it is still expanding, and there appears to be no end in sight. Although scientists cannot observe the entire universe, advancements in technology have allowed us to learn a great deal about space, including our solar system. Among the many planets and celestial bodies, Earth is unique as it is home to many different kinds of organisms.
The Sun plays the most important role in this system, as it is the main source of energy. It provides light and heat, which are essential for maintaining balance within the solar system. Thanks to the Sun, we experience moderate temperatures, day and night, seasonal variations, and the water cycle, all of which support the ecosystem. The planets, including Earth, orbit the Sun, and the distance from the Sun affects the duration of each orbit. For example, Earth takes about 365 days to complete its orbit, while Mercury orbits the Sun in the shortest amount of time, and Neptune takes significantly longer.

M: 우주는 광활하며, 일부 과학자들은 그것이 아예 끝이 없을 수도 있다고 믿습니다. 흥미롭게도 우주는 여전히 팽창하고 있으며, 끝이 보이지 않는 듯 합니다. 과학자들이 우주 전체를 관측할 수는 없지만, 기술의 발전 덕분에 우리는 태양계를 포함하여 우주에 대해 많은 것을 알게 되었습니다. 수많은 행성과 천체 가운데, 지구는 다양한 생명체가 존재하는 유일한 곳이라는 점에서 특별합니다.
태양은 이 시스템에서 가장 중요한 역할을 하는데, 에너지의 주요 원천이기 때문입니다. 태양은 태양계 내의 균형을 유지하는 데 필수적인 빛과 열을 제공합니다. 태양 덕분에 우리는 적당한 온도, 낮과 밤, 계절 변화, 그리고 물의 순환을 경험하는데, 이 모든 것은 생태계를 지탱하는 것들입니다. 지구를 포함한 행성들은 태양 주위를 공전하는데, 태양으로부터의 거리가 각 공전 주기에 영향을 미칩니다. 예를 들어, 지구는 공전을 완료하는 데 365일이 걸리는 반면, 수성은 가장 짧은 시간에 공전을 마치고, 해왕성은 공전을 마치는 데 훨씬 더 오랜 시간이 걸립니다.

37. 기술의 발달은 과학자들에게 어떤 도움을 주었습니까?

(A) 행성의 소리를 들을 수 있도록
(B) 우주의 모든 것을 알 수 있도록
(C) 우주에 대해 훨씬 많이 이해할 수 있도록

38. 다음 중 태양이 하는 중요한 역할이 <u>아닌</u> 것은 무엇입니까?

(A) 지구를 자전시킨다.
(B) 물의 순환을 가능하게 한다.
(C) 기상 패턴을 조절한다.

해설 태양은 지구에 빛, 열, 에너지를 제공하며, 이는 생물체의 생존과 밤낮, 기온 차, 생태계의 유지, 물의 순환, 기상 패턴 등 여러 측면에서 중요한 역할을 한다고 언급되었다. 지구가 태양 주위를 공전한다는 설명은 있었으나, 태양이 지구를 직접 자전시킨다는 내용은 없었기 때문에 답은 (A)이다.

39. 태양을 도는 데 가장 적은 시간이 걸리는 행성은 무엇입니까?

(A) 수성
(B) 지구
(C) 해왕성

Actual Test 2

Reading

1 (B)	2 (C)	3 (A)	4 (A)
5 (A)	6 (B)	7 (A)	8 (C)
9 (C)	10 (A)	11 (B)	12 (B)
13 (C)	14 (C)	15 (B)	16 (A)
17 (C)	18 (A)	19 (C)	20 (B)
21 (A)	22 (B)	23 (B)	24 (C)
25 (C)	26 (C)	27 (B)	28 (C)
29 (A)	30 (C)	31 (C)	32 (B)
33 (A)	34 (A)	35 (A)	36 (A)
37 (C)			

Part 1.

1. 사람들은 이것 위에 섭니다. 보통 네 개의 바퀴가 달린 짧고 평평한 판입니다. 한쪽 발로 땅을 밀면 이것을 타고 앞으로 나아갈 수 있습니다. 이것은 _____ 입니다.

(A) 자전거
(B) 스케이트보드
(C) 오토바이

2. 당신은 아주 긴 줄을 서서 기다리는 중입니다. 앞에는 사람들이 많이 있습니다. 줄이 점점 짧아집니다. 이제 정문이 보입니다. 곧 당신은 _____ 것입니다.

(A) 나가다
(B) 존재하다
(C) 들어가다

3. 당신은 큰 장난감을 사고 싶습니다. 그것을 사기 위해서는 돈이 더 필요합니다. 그 장난감은 가게에 있는 다른 장난감 보다 돈이 많이 듭니다. 이 장난감은 _____.

(A) 비싸다
(B) 가격을 정하다
(C) 지출하다

4. 그녀는 가게 안을 걷고 있습니다. 그녀는 배, 달걀, 우유를 집어 들어 카트에 담고 계산대로 갑니다. 그녀가 하고 있는 것은 무엇입니까?

(A) 식료품 구입
(B) 과일 판매
(C) 카드 교환

5. 작년 당신의 가족은 다른 도시로 이사했습니다. 처음에는 이사하고 싶지 않았지만, 새로운 친구도 사귀고 새로운 학교 생활도 즐기고 있습니다. 다른 도시로 이사한 것은 _____.

   (A) 처음에는 불행 같았지만 실은 행운이었다.
   (B) 어색한 분위기를 깨는 것이었다.
   (C) 낯설고 어색한 일이었다.

6. 로켓이 곧 발사될 예정입니다. 사람들이 카운드 다운을 하고 있습니다. 우주 비행사들이 사람들에게 손을 흔드는 것이 보입니다. 우주 비행사들은 _____ 합니다.

   (A) 정직한
   (B) 용감한
   (C) 겸손한

7. 여성이 동물을 돌보고 있습니다. 아픈 동물들에게 약을 줍니다. 치료를 받은 동물들은 상태가 좋아집니다. 여성은 _____ 입니다.

   (A) 수의사
   (B) 정비사
   (C) 기자

8. 이것은 봉투에 붙이는 것입니다. 이것은 다른 지역이나 국가로 우편물을 보내기 위한 선불 요금입니다. 우체국에서 살 수 있습니다. 이것은 무엇입니까?

   (A) 엽서
   (B) 주소
   (C) 우표

9. 할아버지께서 다른 사람의 말에 귀를 기울이는 것이 중요하다고 말씀하십니다. 그것은 신뢰를 쌓고 서로를 이해하는데 도움이 된다고 합니다. 할아버지는 _____ 이(가) 있습니다.

   (A) 기쁨
   (B) 행동
   (C) 지혜

10. 친구들과 수영장에서 놀고 있습니다. 수영장에는 많은 튜브가 있습니다. 그것들이 물 위에 있는 것을 볼 수 있습니다. 튜브는 _____ 있습니다.

    (A) 떠 있다
    (B) 떨어지고 있다
    (C) 인사하고 있다

11. 새들이 부지런히 나뭇가지, 나뭇잎, 풀을 모으고 있습니다. 새들은 나무 위에 작은 집을 만들고 있습니다. 이것은 _____ 입니다.

    (A) 굴
    (B) 둥지
    (C) 연못

Part 2.

[12-15] 아래를 읽고, 12-15번 질문에 답하세요.

Martins School Drama Club
일주일 동안 펼쳐지는 연극의 마법!

이번 주, 우리 동아리 학생들이 모든 학생과 학부모님을 위해 유명한 연극과 뮤지컬을 공연합니다.
오셔서 재능 있는 학생들을 응원하고 멋진 공연을 즐기세요!

월요일	《한여름 밤의 꿈》	오후 5시	강당
화요일	《이상한 나라의 앨리스》	오후 5시 30분	연극 스튜디오
수요일	《정글북》	오후 6시	강당
목요일	《크리스마스 캐럴》	오후 6시 30분	체육관
금요일	《피터 팬》	오후 4시 30분	연극 스튜디오

입장료
연극 동아리 회원: 3달러
연극 동아리 회원 외 학생: 5달러
학부모: 10달러
모든 티켓 수익은 자선단체에 기부됩니다.

모든 좌석은 선착순이니, 일찍 도착하세요!

12. 다음 중 일정에 포함되지 않은 연극은 무엇입니까?

    (A) 이상한 나라의 앨리스
    (B) 헨젤과 그레텔
    (C) 크리스마스 캐럴

13. 목요일 공연 장소는 어디입니까?

    (A) 연극 스튜디오
    (B) 강당
    (C) 체육관

14. 티켓 수익금이 사용될 가능성이 높은 곳은 어디입니까?

    (A) 수영장
    (B) 드라마 클럽
    (C) 환경 재단

15. 이 안내문이 강조하는 것은 무엇입니까?

    (A) 연극 중 하나에 참여할 것
    (B) 가능한 빨리 도착할 것
    (C) 연극 준비를 도울 것

[16-17] 이메일을 읽고, 16-17번 질문에 답하세요.

받는 사람: Luke 선생님
보낸 사람: Tiffany 선생님
제목: 학교 축제

안녕하세요, Luke 선생님. Tiffany입니다. 신나는 소식이 있습니다. 올해 학교 축제의 주제가 Harry Potter라는 얘기 들으셨나요? 학교 축제를 더 재미있게 만들 수 있는 흥미로운 아이디어가 몇 개 있어요. 학생들을 각기 다른 기숙사로 배정하는 걸 생각 중입니다. 학생들이 호그와트 교복을 입고 지팡이도 하나씩 가지고 있으면 정말 멋질 것 같아요. 또한 하루 종일 영화 속 음악들을 틀어두는 건 어떨까요? 미술 선생님이신 만큼 학교 전체를 꾸미느라 많이 바쁘실 것 같습니다. 제가 도울 수 있는 일이 있다면 말씀해 주세요.

감사합니다.

Tiffany 드림

16. Tiffany 선생님이 제안한 아이디어가 <u>아닌</u> 것은 무엇입니까?

(A) 지팡이 만들기

(B) 호그와트 교복 입기

(C) 음악 듣기

17. Tiffany 선생님이 편지를 쓴 이유는 무엇입니까?

(A) 올해 학교 축제에 대해 Luke 선생님이 기대하고 있는지 물어보기 위해

(B) Luke 선생님에게 학교를 함께 꾸며달라고 부탁하기 위해

(C) Luke 선생님이 학교를 꾸미는 데 도움이 필요한지 물어보기 위해

[18-19] 이메일을 읽고, 18–19번 질문에 답하세요.

받는 사람: 학생 전체
보낸 사람: Vivian 선생님
제목: 요리 수업 안내

여러분 모두 다음 주 요리 수업에서 무엇을 만들지 궁금해하고 있었죠? 가장 인기 있었던 메뉴 세 가지는 스파게티 미트볼, 캐러멜 애플 케이크, 브로콜리 수프였어요. 그 중에서 가장 많은 표를 받은 것은 스파게티 미트볼이었습니다. 다음 주 목요일에 요리 수업이 있으니, 재료를 꼭 챙겨 오세요! 요리 수업은 단순히 재미있는 시간일 뿐만 아니라, 매일 먹는 식사에서 더 건강한 선택을 하는 것의 중요성도 배울 수 있는 기회가 될 거예요. 영양가 있는 식사를 하는 것은 건강하고 균형 잡힌 식사를 위해 중요합니다.
좋은 하루 보내길 바랍니다.

Vivian 선생님 보냄

18. 다음 주 목요일에 학생들이 요리할 것은 무엇입니까?

(A) 스파게티와 미트볼

(B) 캐러멜 애플 케이크

(C) 브로콜리 수프

19. Vivian 선생님이 학생들에게 배우길 바라는 것은 무엇입니까?

(A) 훌륭한 요리사가 되는 법

(B) 다양한 메뉴를 요리하는 법

(C) 균형 잡힌 식사의 중요성

[20-22] 안내문을 읽고, 20–22번 질문에 답하세요.

점토로 창의력 키우기

점토를 가지고 놀며 재미있는 물건을 만드는 것은 창의력을 키우는 훌륭한 방법입니다. 점토는 원하는 대로 굴리고, 자르고, 모양을 만들 수 있습니다. 이렇게 하여 점토 덩어리를 독특한 물건으로 바꿀 수 있습니다. 오늘은 여러분만의 디자인으로 컵을 만들어 보겠습니다.

준비물:
점토 (원하는 색상)
밀대
플라스틱 칼
이쑤시개

만드는 방법:
1. 점토 가지고 놀기. 점토를 주물러서 부드럽게 만드세요.
2. 밀대로 점토를 평평하고 매끄럽게 만드세요.
3. 점토를 큰 직사각형, 작은 원, 길쭉한 선의 세 가지 모양으로 자르세요.
4. 컵 옆면: 큰 직사각형을 말아서 컵 모양을 만들고 끝을 눌러 붙입니다.
5. 작은 원을 컵 바닥에 붙이고 살살 눌러 몸통과 붙입니다.
6. 손잡이: 길쭉한 선을 'c'자 모양으로 구부립니다.
7. 손잡이의 끝을 컵 옆면에 붙입니다.
8. 손가락과 이쑤시개를 사용해 컵에 자신만의 디자인을 꾸밉니다.
9. 점토 위에 종이 호일을 덮습니다.
   – 이제 오븐에 구울 준비가 되었습니다! (꼭 선생님의 도움을 받으세요!)

20. 점토를 여러 모양으로 자른 다음에는 무엇을 해야 합니까?

(A) 점토를 주물러서 부드럽게 만든다.

(B) 직사각형을 말아서 컵 모양으로 만든다.

(C) 이쑤시개를 사용해 점토를 꾸민다.

21. 작은 원은 어디에 붙여야 합니까?

(A) 점토의 바닥

(B) 점토의 옆면

(C) 점토의 중앙

22. 컵을 종이 호일로 덮은 후에는 무엇을 합니까?

(A) 식히기

(B) 굽기

(C) 부드럽게 만들기

[23-25] 다음을 읽고, 23–25번 질문에 답하세요.

이쑤시개로 창의력 키우기

이쑤시개는 다양한 용도로 사용할 수 있습니다. 요리, 탑 쌓기, 청소, 또는 다양한 모양을 만드는 데 쓸 수 있어요.
많은 사람들이 이쑤시개를 이용해 다양한 물건을 만들어 창의성을 발휘합니다. 오늘은 고슴도치를 만드는 방법을 배울 거예요!

만드는게 정말 쉬워서 고슴도치 가족 전체를 만들어 볼 수도 있겠네요!

준비물:
점토 (연한 갈색)
이쑤시개 (약 20~30개)
색종이 (눈과 코를 위한 검은색, 발을 위한 분홍색)
가위와 풀

만드는 방법:
– 점토를 주물러서 부드럽게 만듭니다.
– 타원형으로 점토를 빚어 고슴도치 몸통을 만듭니다.
– 몸통의 한쪽을 살짝 꼬집어 얼굴 모양을 만듭니다.
– 검은 색종이로 작은 원 3개를 잘라 눈과 코를 만듭니다.
– 분홍색 색종이로 작은 타원 4개를 잘라 다리를 만듭니다.
– 눈과 코를 고슴도치 얼굴에 붙입니다.
– 다리는 몸통 아래쪽에 붙입니다.
– 이쑤시개를 점토에 꽂아 가시를 만듭니다.
– 이쑤시개 끝이 뾰족하니 조심해서 사용하세요.

23. 색종이를 자르는 이유는 무엇입니까?

(A) 몸을 감싸기 위해
(B) 눈과 코를 만들기 위해
(C) 가시를 만들기 위해

24. 색종이를 자른 후에는 무엇을 해야 합니까?

(A) 고슴도치 몸통의 한쪽을 꼬집는다.
(B) 점토 안에 이쑤시개를 꽂는다.
(C) 자른 모양을 고슴도치 몸에 붙인다.

25. 분홍색 타원형 모양은 어디에 붙여야 합니까?

(A) 고슴도치 얼굴
(B) 고슴도치 몸통
(C) 고슴도치 발

[26-29] 다음을 읽고, 26–29번 질문에 답하세요.

"Violet, 우리가 과학 프로젝트 같은 팀이라니 믿기지 않아!" Daisy가 외쳤습니다. "나도 정말 기뻐! 드디어 같은 팀이 되었어! 우리 학교 역사상 최고의 프로젝트를 만들어보자!!" Violet이 대답했습니다.

두 여학생은 학교에서 태양계에 대해 배우고 있습니다. 수성, 금성, 지구, 화성, 목성, 토성, 천왕성, 해왕성에 대해 자세히 배웠습니다. 이번 프로젝트는 그들만의 행성을 만드는 것입니다. 이 행성에는 세 가지 다른 행성의 특징을 최소한 하나씩 포함해야 합니다.

"우리 행성을 수성처럼 만들어 보는 건 어때? 태양에 가장 가까운 위치에 두면 재미있을 것 같아." Daisy가 말했습니다.
"좋은 생각이야. 그 다음에 우리 행성을 목성처럼 제일 큰 행성으로 만들어 볼까?" Violet이 제안했습니다.
"그러자. 목성보다 두 배 더 크게 만들자. 너무 커서 반 친구들이 깜짝 놀랄 거야." Daisy가 외쳤습니다.

"좋은데. 색깔은 어떻게 할까? 색깔에 대해 생각해 봤는데, 금성처럼 노란색, 화성처럼 빨간색, 아니면 해왕성처럼 짙은 파란색?" Violet이 말했습니다.
"흠, 네가 좋아하는 색이 나랑 같은 거 알아. 그럼 파란색으로 할까?" Daisy가 물었습니다.
"완벽해! 우리 행성의 특징은 정했으니까, 내일 학교 끝나고 만나서 만들까?" Violet이 제안했습니다.
내일 해야 할 일을 생각하며 Daisy가 말했습니다. "먼저 엄마한테 물어봐야 해서. 오늘 밤까지 알려줘도 괜찮아?"
"물론이지. 정해지면 전화 줘. 그리고 행성 만들 재료 사러 시장에도 꼭 가야 해." Violet이 말했습니다.
"맞아. 오늘 밤에 전화할게!" Daisy가 손을 흔들며 말했습니다.

26. 학생들은 과학 프로젝트를 위해 무엇을 해야 합니까?

(A) 태양계에 관한 발표
(B) 자신이 공부한 행성에 대한 개인 프로젝트
(C) 자신만의 행성 만들기

해설 Violet과 Daisy가 학교에서 과학 프로젝트를 함께 하기로 했으며, 서로의 파트너가 되어 매우 기뻐한다는 내용이 언급되었다. 프로젝트 주제는 자신들이 선택한 행성을 만드는 것이며, 본문에 그 방법에 관한 설명이 포함되어 있기 때문에 답은 (C)이다.

27. Violet과 Daisy는 행성을 만들 때 고려하고 있는 세 행성은 무엇입니까?

(A) 수성, 금성, 해왕성
(B) 수성, 해왕성, 목성
(C) 수성, 목성, 화성

28. 그들은 행성을 어떤 색으로 칠할 가능성이 높습니까?

(A) 노란색
(B) 빨간색
(C) 파란색

29. Daisy는 왜 오늘 밤 Violet에게 전화하려고 합니까?

(A) 내일 만날 수 있는지 여부를 말해주기 위해
(B) 시장에서 필요한 재료를 다 샀는지 알려주기 위해
(C) 내일 시장에 전화하라고 상기시키기 위해

[30-33] 다음을 읽고, 30–33번 질문에 답하세요.

따뜻한 토요일 오후, Aaron과 그의 가족이 매년 찍는 가족사진을 찍기 위해 사진관에 막 도착했습니다. 모든 가족들이 도착했고, 모두 사진을 찍을 생각에 들떠 있었습니다.

"엄마, 나 중간에 앉아도 돼? 할아버지 옆에 앉고 싶어. 지난번엔 Daisy가 중간에 앉았으니까, 이번엔 내가 중간에 앉아야 공평하잖아!" Aaron이 외쳤습니다.
"그럼, 물론이지! 그런데 Aaron, 사진 찍기 전에 셔츠 좀 안으로 넣어

줄래?" Aaron의 엄마가 말했습니다.

Aaron은 재빨리 셔츠를 넣고는 사진 부스 가운데로 가며 말했습니다. "Daisy, 이번엔 내가 가운데야!"

"괜찮아. 난 아빠 옆에 설 거야. 아빠가 나 어부바해주기로 했거든." Daisy가 대답했습니다.

사진사가 카메라를 들면서 말했습니다. "다들 준비되셨나요? 이제 10분 안에 사진 찍을게요! 모두 모여주세요!"

곧 Aaron의 가족들이 모여 최고의 미소를 지었습니다. Aaron은 가족사진 찍는 걸 정말 좋아했습니다. 가족들 사이의 사랑과 유대감을 느낄 수 있었기 때문입니다.

"가족사진 찍는 것은 내가 가장 좋아하는 일 중 하나야. 서로의 추억을 떠올리게 해주니까." Aaron의 아빠가 말했습니다.

"나도! 내가 해가 지날수록 얼마나 자라고 변하는지 보는 것도 좋아." Daisy가 외쳤습니다.

---

30. Aaron의 가족은 얼마나 자주 가족사진을 찍습니까?

(A) 매주
(B) 매달
(C) 매년

31. Aaron은 왜 엄마에게 중간에 앉아도 되냐고 물어봤습니까?

(A) Daisy 옆에 앉고 싶어서
(B) 아빠 옆에 앉고 싶어서
(C) 할아버지 옆에 앉고 싶어서

32. Aaron이 가족사진을 찍기 전에 해야 할 일은 무엇입니까?

(A) 할아버지에게 자신이 옆에 앉을 거라고 말하기
(B) 셔츠를 바지 안으로 넣기
(C) 사진사에게 준비되었다고 말하기

33. Daisy가 가족사진 찍는 것을 좋아하는 이유는 무엇입니까?

(A) 자신이 변화하고 성장하는 모습을 볼 수 있어서
(B) 예쁜 옷을 입고 화장을 하는 것이 좋아서
(C) 사진 찍는 것을 좋아해서

[34-35] 다음을 읽고, 34-35번 질문에 답하세요.

동물계는 다양한 동물 종들로 가득하며, 대부분은 서로 다른 동물 무리로 분류됩니다. 여러 유형 중에서, 동물들은 먹는 방식에 따라 세 가지로 나뉩니다. 첫 번째는 육식동물입니다. 이 동물들은 고기, 즉 다른 동물을 먹습니다. 하지만 식단을 조절하기 위해 식물을 먹기도 합니다. 육식동물은 날카로운 이빨을 가지고 있어 먹잇감을 사냥할 때 사용합니다. 늑대, 사자, 호랑이가 이 유형의 대표적인 예입니다. 식물을 먹는 동물은 초식동물이라고 부릅니다. 이들은 식물을 잘게 부수고 씹기 위해 평평한 이빨을 가지고 있습니다. 그 예로는 코끼리, 기린, 낙타가 있습니다. 마지막으로 모든 것을 먹는 잡식동물이 있습니다. 잡식동물은 음식을 찢고 씹을 수 있도록 날카로운 이빨과 평평한 이빨을 모두 가지고 있습니다. 잘 알려진 예로는 곰, 침팬지가 있고, 당연히 인간도 여기에 속합니다.

---

34. 본문에서는 동물을 어떤 기준으로 나눕니까?

(A) 먹는 습성
(B) 자는 습성
(C) 사냥하는 습성

35. 본문에서 언급되지 않은 이빨의 종류는 무엇입니까?

(A) 사랑니
(B) 날카로운 이빨
(C) 평평한 이빨

해설 육식 동물이 고기를 잘 먹을 수 있도록 날카로운 이빨을 가지고 있고, 초식 동물은 식물을 갈아 부드럽게 씹기 위해 납작한 이빨을 가지고 있다고 설명한다. 이런 이빨 모양은 각 동물의 식습관에 맞게 발달한 것으로, 보기에 나온 사랑니는 이에 해당하지 않아 정답이 될 수 없다. 따라서 답은 (A)이다.

[36-37] 다음을 읽고, 36-37번 질문에 답하세요.

Helen Keller는 세계에서 가장 유명하고 존경받는 영웅이자 사회운동가 중 한 명입니다. 그녀는 여느 평범한 아이로 태어났지만, 생후 19개월이 되었을 때 매우 심하게 병을 앓아 시력과 청력을 잃었습니다. 사람들과 소통할 수 없게 되자, 그녀는 생각과 감정을 표현하는 데 어려움을 겪었고 자주 좌절했습니다. 그녀는 여섯 살이 되었을 때 Anne Sullivan 선생님을 만났고, 둘은 평생 동안 우정을 나누었습니다. Anne 선생님은 Helen의 손바닥에 글자를 써서 단어를 가르쳤습니다. Helen은 또한 다른 사람의 입술을 만지고 목의 떨림을 느끼면서 말하는 법을 배웠습니다. 그녀는 또한 글자, 기호, 숫자를 나타내는 볼록한 점으로 된 체계인 점자를 읽는 법도 배웠습니다. 이후 Helen은 사회운동가가 되어 다른 사람들을 도왔습니다. 그녀는 여성과 모든 사람들의 평등한 권리를 지지했으며, 전 세계를 다니며 많은 사람들에게 어려움을 극복하도록 격려하는 연설을 했습니다.

---

36. Helen Keller가 어린 시절 잃지 않은 감각은 무엇입니까?

(A) 촉각
(B) 청각
(C) 시각

37. Helen Keller는 어떻게 전 세계 사람들을 도왔습니까?

(A) Anne Sullivan의 선생님이 되었다.
(B) 점자를 만들었다.
(C) 사람들이 어려움을 극복하도록 도왔다.

1 (B)	2 (A)	3 (B)	4 (A)
5 (A)	6 (B)	7 (C)	8 (C)
9 (B)	10 (A)	11 (B)	12 (C)
13 (C)	14 (B)	15 (B)	16 (A)
17 (A)	18 (A)	19 (A)	20 (C)
21 (B)	22 (C)	23 (C)	24 (C)
25 (B)	26 (C)	27 (A)	28 (B)
29 (B)	30 (B)	31 (C)	32 (B)
33 (C)	34 (A)	35 (C)	36 (C)
37 (B)	38 (C)	39 (B)	

Part 1.

1.
W: Listen to a teacher.
W: We are going to do a group presentation this week. I want all of you to pick a piece of paper from this box. On it will be the name of your partner.
W: What did the teacher tell the students to do?

W: 선생님이 하는 얘기를 들어보세요.
W: 이번 주에는 그룹 발표가 있을 예정입니다. 이 상자에서 모두 종이를 한 장씩 뽑으세요. 종이에 여러분의 파트너 이름이 적혀 있을 거예요.
W: 선생님이 학생들에게 하라고 한 것은 무엇입니까?

2.
W: Listen to a girl.
G: Mom, I need a new pair of trainers. I've been wearing these for two years, and not only have I grown out of them, but they look worn out. Can we go get new ones?
W: What did the girl ask her mother to do?

W: 소녀가 하는 얘기를 들어보세요.
G: 엄마, 나 새 운동화가 필요해요. 이건 2년 동안 신었는데, 발도 커졌고, 보기에도 낡았어요. 새 신발 사러 가면 안돼요?
W: 소녀가 엄마에게 요청한 것은 무엇입니까?

3.
W: Listen to a girl.
G: Grandma, the macarons we made were so delicious. I took them to school and gave them to my friends. They loved them! Can we make some more today? Mom plans to go grocery shopping later, and I can buy the ingredients when I go with her.
W: What did the girl ask her grandmother to do?

W: 소녀가 하는 얘기를 들어보세요.
G: 할머니, 할머니랑 함께 만들었던 마카롱 정말 맛있었어요. 학교에

가져가서 친구들에게 나눠줬더니 다들 정말 좋아했어요. 오늘 또 마카롱 만들 수 있어요? 엄마가 있다가 장보러 가실 건데 저도 따라가서 재료를 살 수 있어요.
W: 소녀가 할머니에게 요청한 것은 무엇입니까?

4.
W: Listen to a teacher.
M: Please don't forget to tell your parents about next Wednesday's sports day. Parents should park their cars in front of the science building, not in the school parking lot. The parking zone is under construction, so there isn't any parking space.
W: What did the teacher tell the students to do?

W: 선생님이 하는 얘기를 들어보세요.
M: 잊지 말고 부모님께 다음 주 수요일에 있을 체육대회에 대해 말씀드리세요. 부모님 차량은 학교 주차장이 아닌 과학관 앞에 주차해야 합니다. 주차 구역이 공사 중이라 사용할 수 없습니다.
W: 선생님이 학생들에게 하라고 한 것은 무엇입니까?

5.
W: Listen to a teacher.
M: The cafeteria will be closed again tomorrow, so please don't forget to bring a packed lunch. For those who can't get lunch from home, please come forward and write your name on this piece of paper. The school will provide a lunchbox for you. There will be a charge of five dollars, and you have to pay in advance.
W: What did the teacher tell the students to do?

W: 선생님이 하는 얘기를 들어보세요.
M: 내일 또 급식실이 문을 닫을 예정이니, 잊지 말고 도시락 챙겨 오세요. 집에서 점심을 가져올 수 없는 학생은 앞으로 나와서 이 종이에 이름을 적으세요. 학교에서 도시락을 준비해 줄 거예요. 비용은 5달러이고, 선불로 결제해야 합니다.
W: 선생님이 학생들에게 하라고 한 것은 무엇입니까?

6.
W: Listen to a teacher.
W: Friendship is one of the most important elements for all people. It helps people to overcome hardships in life and share special memories. It's not the length of time two people have known each other; it's the depth of thoughts that bring each other close. This is why today, we will write a letter to a friend and tell them how much we care. Don't forget to think deeply and be honest about your feelings.
W: What did the teacher tell the students to do?

W: 선생님이 하는 얘기를 들어보세요.
W: 우정은 모든 사람에게 가장 중요한 요소 중 하나입니다. 우정은 사람이 인생의 어려움을 극복하고 특별한 추억을 나누는 데 도움이 됩니다. 서로를 얼마나 오래 알았느냐보다, 생각의 깊이가 서로를 더 가깝게 만듭니다. 그래서 오늘은 친구에게 편지를 써서 얼마나 그 친구가 중요한지 마음을 전할 거예요. 깊이 생각하고 솔직한 마음을 담으세요.
W: 선생님이 학생들에게 하라고 한 것은 무엇입니까?

7.

M: Listen to a conversation between two friends. Listen for the answer to this question.

B: I'm not doing well in my history class.

G: Have you tried talking to the teacher?

B: Not yet. Maybe I need a study partner.

G: If you want, I can study with you.

B: That sounds great. When can you help me?

G: Well, I have band practice in 5 minutes. So how about studying tomorrow after school?

B: OK, that sounds good. Do you want to meet at the school library?

G: Yes, see you tomorrow.

M: What will the girl probably do next?

M: 두 친구 사이의 대화를 듣고 질문에 답하세요.

B: 나 역사 수업에서 성적이 안 나와

G: 선생님께 말씀드려 봤어?

B: 아직, 아마 공부 파트너가 필요한 것 같아.

G: 네가 원하면 같이 공부해 줄게.

B: 좋아. 언제 도와줄 수 있어?

G: 음, 5분 뒤에 밴드 연습이 있어. 내일 방과 후에 공부하는 건 어때?

B: 좋아, 학교 도서관에서 만날까?

G: 그래. 내일 보자.

M: 소녀가 곧 할 것 같은 것은 무엇입니까?

(A) 선생님과 상담하기
(B) 소년과 공부하기
(C) 밴드 연습하러 가기

8.

M: Listen to a conversation between a mother and her daughter. Listen for the answer to this question.

G: Mom, have you seen my goggles? They're not in my swimming bag.

W: Are you sure? I'm certain that I put them in your bag last night. Can you look again?

G: Ah ha! I found them. They were underneath the towel.

W: Good, are you ready for your swim practice?

G: In a minute. Can I go get my camera? You promised to record my practice today.

W: Don't worry, I've already got it.

M: What promise did the girl's mom make?

M: 엄마와 딸 사이의 대화를 듣고 질문에 답하세요.

G: 엄마, 내 물안경 봤어요? 수영 가방에 없어요.

W: 정말? 어젯밤 분명히 넣어뒀는데. 다시 찾아볼래?

G: 앗! 찾았어요. 수건 밑에 있었어요.

W: 다행이네. 수영 연습할 준비됐어?

G: 잠시만요. 카메라 가져와도 돼요? 오늘 연습 촬영해 주신다고 약속하셨잖아요.

W: 걱정 마. 벌써 챙겨놨어.

M: 엄마가 딸에게 한 약속은 무엇입니까?

(A) 수영 가방 미리 챙겨 주기
(B) 딸의 물건 제대로 찾아주기
(C) 딸의 연습을 촬영해 주기

9.

M: Listen to a conversation between a father and his son. Listen for the answer to this question.

M: Hey David, can you give me a hand in cleaning out the garage?

B: No problem! Where should I start?

M: Do you see those paint cans and broken tools over there?

B: Yes, should I put them in the trash?

M: Only the paint cans, but remember to recycle them.

B: What about the broken tools?

M: I'm going to take a look at them first and fix the ones that can be repaired.

M: What does the boy agree to do?

M: 아빠와 아들 사이의 대화를 듣고 질문에 답하세요.

M: 데이비드, 차고 정리 좀 도와줄래?

B: 네. 무엇부터 하면 될까요?

M: 저기 페인트 통이랑 고장 난 도구들 보이니?

B: 네. 쓰레기통에 버릴까요?

M: 페인트 통만 버리렴, 재활용 꼭 하고.

B: 고장 난 도구들은요?

M: 먼저 한번 살펴보고 고칠 수 있으면 고칠 거야.

M: 아들은 무엇을 하기로 동의했습니까?

(A) 고장 난 도구를 버리기로
(B) 페인트 통을 재활용 통에 넣기로
(C) 아빠가 고장 난 도구를 수리하는 것을 돕기로

10.

M: Listen to a conversation between a mother and her daughter. Listen for the answer to this question.

G: Mom, all of these dresses for Sara's birthday party are beautiful. I can't pick one.

W: It's hard for me too. All of them looked great on you.

G: How about the blue one I tried on first? It would match my headband.

W: The blue one looked good, but since it's winter, how about a warmer color?

G: Then the yellow one? It would look great with my earrings.

W: The yellow one suited you too. But didn't you say the pink dress goes perfectly with your shoes?

G: I did, but I made up my mind. Since Grandpa gave me the headband as a present, I'll go with the first choice.

M: What will the girl wear to Sara's birthday party?

M: 엄마와 딸 사이의 대화를 듣고 질문에 답하세요.

G: 엄마, Sara 생일파티에서 입을 드레스들이 모두 너무 예뻐요. 하나만 고를 수가 없어요.

W: 엄마도 마찬가지야. 다 너에게 잘 어울리는구나.

G: 처음 입었던 파란 드레스는 어때요? 제 머리띠랑 잘 어울릴 것 같아요.

W: 파란 드레스가 잘 어울리긴 했는데, 겨울이니까 좀 더 따뜻한 색깔은 어때?

G: 노란 드레스는 어때요? 귀걸이랑 잘 어울릴 것 같아요.

W: 노란색도 잘 어울렸지. 그런데 핑크색 드레스가 신발이랑 완벽하게 어울린다고 하지 않았었니?

G: 맞아요. 그런데 마음을 정했어요. 할아버지가 머리띠를 선물해 주셨으니까, 첫 번째로 입어봤던 드레스로 할게요.

M: 딸이 Sara's 생일 파티에 입을 드레스는 무엇인가요?

(A) 파란색 드레스
(B) 노란색 드레스
(C) 핑크색 드레스

11.

M: Listen to a conversation between a girl and her teacher. Listen for the answer to this question.

W: It's Christmas soon, so we're looking for volunteers who can help decorate the school.

G: I would love to help! What would we be doing?

W: First, we need students to make paper ornaments, snowflakes, trees, and maybe some flowers.

G: That sounds fun! Anything else?

W: We also need to decorate the Christmas trees. We're planning to have one for each classroom.

G: I'm definitely signing up for that one. Can we bring our decorations from home?

W: Of course you may. The more, the better!

M: What does the girl say she will do?

M: 소녀와 선생님 사이의 대화를 듣고 질문에 답하세요.

W: 곧 크리스마스라서, 학교를 장식하는 걸 도와줄 자원자를 찾고 있어요.

G: 제가 하고 싶어요. 어떤 일을 하게 되나요?

W: 먼저, 종이 장식, 눈송이, 나무, 그리고 어쩌면 꽃 같은 걸 만들 학생이 필요해요.

G: 재미있을 것 같아요. 다른 것도 있나요?

W: 크리스마스트리도 장식할 계획이에요. 교실마다 하나씩 둘 계획이거든요.

G: 저는 무조건 신청할게요. 집에서 장식품을 가져와도 되나요?

W: 당연하죠. 많으면 많을수록 좋답니다.

M: 소녀가 하겠다고 말한 것은 무엇입니까?

(A) 종이 장식 만들기
(B) 크리스마스트리 장식하기
(C) 크리스마스 장식품 사기

12.

M: Listen to a conversation between a father and his son. Listen for the answer to this question.

B: Dad, you look busy. What are you making?

M: Hey, kiddo, I'm building a birdhouse. Do you want to help?

B: Sure! What can I do?

M: I've already attached the sides and floor of the birdhouse. All it needs is a little paint.

B: How about the roof? Doesn't it need a roof?

M: You're right! I nearly forgot. How about you help me nail it on?

B: Sure. Should I hold it like this?

M: That's right; thanks, Arthur.

B: What if we paint the birdhouse blue or red?

M: How about green? It will help birds to blend in with the leaves and the trees.

M: What will the boy do first?

M: 아빠와 아들 사이의 대화를 듣고 질문에 답하세요.

B: 아빠, 바쁘신 것 같은데 뭐 만들고 계세요?

M: 아들, 새집 만들고 있지. 좀 도와줄래?

B: 네, 뭘 하면 될까요?

M: 옆면이랑 바닥은 이미 붙였고, 약간의 페인트칠만 하면 돼.

B: 지붕은요? 지붕도 있어야 하지 않아요?

M: 맞다. 까먹을 뻔했네. 지붕을 못질해서 고정하는 것 좀 도와줄래?

B: 이렇게 들고 있으면 돼요?

M: 맞아. 고맙다, 아서.

B: 새집을 파랑이나 빨강으로 칠하는 건 어때요?

M: 초록은 어때? 새들이 나뭇잎과 나무에 섞여 들기 쉽게.

M: 아들이 처음으로 하게 될 일은 무엇입니까?

(A) 새집을 초록색으로 칠하기
(B) 새집을 파란색으로 칠하기
(C) 새집 지붕 못질해서 고정하기

13.

M: Listen to a conversation between a mother and her daughter. Listen for the answer to this question.

W: I'm off to pick up your sister.

G: When will you be back?

W: Your sister needs a new bag for school, so we're going to the mall first.

G: You're going to the mall? Can I come with you?

W: Of course you can. Do you need anything?

G: I want to check out the new headphones.

W: Sure, and while we're there, why don't we get you a new keyboard? I know you were having trouble with typing.

G: It's OK; after Dad fixed it, it works fine.

M: Why does the girl want to go to the mall?

M: 엄마와 딸 사이의 대화를 듣고 질문에 답하세요.

W: 언니 좀 데리러 갈게.

G: 언제 오실 거예요?

W: 언니가 학교에 쓸 가방이 필요해서 먼저 쇼핑몰에 들를 거야.

G: 쇼핑몰 가세요? 저도 같이 가도 돼요?

W: 물론이지. 필요한 것 있어?

G: 새 헤드폰 좀 구경하고 싶어요.

W: 그래. 가는 김에 새 키보드도 하나 살까? 타이핑하는 데 불편하다며.

G: 괜찮아요. 아빠가 고쳐 주신 이후로는 잘 작동해요.

M: 딸은 왜 쇼핑몰에 가고 싶어 합니까?

(A) 새 가방을 사고 싶어서

(B) 새 키보드를 사고 싶어서

(C) 새 헤드폰을 구경하고 싶어서

14.

M: Listen to a conversation between two students. Listen for the answer to this question.

B: Ha Young, did you hear that there is going to be a carnival this Saturday?

G: I sure did. I'm super excited!

B: Do you remember the carnival last year?
Apparently, it's going to be even bigger this year.

G: Really, I wonder if there's going to be a Ferris wheel. They didn't have one last time.

B: Yes, it would be great to have one. But, I can't wait to ride the bumper cars and get my face painted.

G: I loved that last year, too, but I'm unsure about the bumper cars. They looked scary.

B: I'm sure there are going to be other fun things to do! I hope Saturday comes soon!

M: What does the girl NOT want to do?

M: 두 학생 사이의 대화를 듣고 질문에 답하세요.

B: 하영, 이번 토요일에 축제 있다는 얘기 들었어?

G: 들었어. 완전 신나!

B: 작년 축제 기억나? 이번에는 더 크게 열릴거래.

G: 진짜? 이번엔 관람차도 있을까? 작년엔 없었잖아.

B: 그러게. 있었으면 좋겠다. 난 범퍼카 타고 페이스 페인팅 받는 거 너무 기대돼.

G: 페이스 페인팅은 나도 좋아했는데, 범퍼카는 좀 무서워 보였어.

B: 다른 재밌는 것도 많을 거야. 토요일이 빨리 왔으면 좋겠다.

M: 소녀가 하고 싶어 하지 <u>않는</u> 것은 무엇입니까?

(A) 관람차 타기

(B) 범퍼카 타기

(C) 페이스 페인팅 받기

15.

M: Listen to a conversation between two students at school. Listen for the answer to this question.

B: I think math is so difficult. I have a hard time doing math homework.

G: If you want, I can help you. Math is my favorite subject. It's one of the easiest subjects for me.
We can study together, and I can help you.

B: Great! Thank you. When do you want to get together to study?

G: How about today after school?

B: I have basketball practice after school. Can we do it in the evening?

G: OK. Then see you at the library at 7.

B: Can we make it 8? I usually eat dinner around 7.

G: OK, see you later then.

M: What does the girl agree to do?

M: 학교에서 두 학생 사이의 대화를 듣고 질문에 답하세요.

B: 나는 수학이 너무 어려운 것 같아. 수학 숙제하는 게 힘들어.

G: 원하면 내가 도와줄게. 수학은 내가 제일 좋아하는 과목이거든. 나한테는 제일 쉬운 과목 중 하나야. 같이 공부하면 내가 도와줄 수 있어.

B: 정말? 고마워. 언제 같이 공부할까?

G: 오늘 방과 후는 어때?

B: 방과 후엔 농구 연습이 있어. 저녁에 하면 안될까?

G: 좋아. 7시에 도서관에서 만나자.

B: 8시는 어때? 7시에 저녁을 먹어서.

G: 그래. 그때 보자.

M: 소녀는 무엇을 하기로 동의했습니까?

(A) 방과 후 스포츠 연습하기

(B) 저녁에 함께 공부하기

(C) 8시에 저녁 먹기

Part 3

16.

B: Hi, Bill, this is Tom. Listen, we can't use my dad's beach house this weekend. He said he's going to rent it to someone. I'm really sorry. I know you were really looking forward to going to the beach. Maybe we can use the beach house in a few weeks. I'll let you know.

M: Why did Tom call?

B: 안녕, Bill. 나 Tom이야. 있잖아, 이번 주말에 우리 아빠 해변 별장을 못 쓰게 됐어. 아빠가 다른 누군가에게 빌려주신대. 정말 미안해. 너 해변에 가는 거 많이 기대하고 있었는데. 아마 몇 주 후엔 쓸 수 있을 거야. 그때 다시 알려줄게.

M: Tom은 왜 전화했나요?

(A) 해변 여행을 취소하려고
(B) 해변에 가자고 제안하자고
(C) 여름휴가를 계획하려고

17.

M: Hello, Sue. This is Mr. Brown, your homeroom teacher. Due to heavy snow, school will begin at 10 a.m. tomorrow. The snowfall today was very heavy, so it will be impossible to start school at the usual time. And please be aware that the school bus schedule will also be delayed by one hour. Be careful, and see you tomorrow at school.

M: Why did Mr. Brown call?

M: 여보세요, Sue. 담임인 Brown 선생님이야. 폭설 때문에 내일은 학교가 오전 10시에 시작해. 오늘 눈이 너무 많이 왔잖아. 그래서 평소 시간에 학교를 시작하는 것은 불가능할 것 같아. 그리고 스쿨버스 시간도 한 시간 늦춰질 예정이니 참고해. 조심하고 내일 봐.

M: Brown은 왜 전화했나요?

(A) 학교가 늦게 시작된다는 것을 알리기 위해
(B) 일기예보를 전하기 위해
(C) 버스 시간표에 대해 묻기 위해

18.

B: Sunny, before I answer your question, I want to congratulate you on winning the photography contest. I saw your pictures at the school auditorium, and they truly stood out from the rest. All the other students gathered around to see your work. It was amazing. About the favor you asked me, of course, I'm able to help with your history homework. How about we meet at the public library in an hour? I'll head there now. Also, make sure to bring your notebook. We will need it to do some research.

M: Where did the boy tell the girl to meet?

B: Sunny, 네 질문에 답하기 전에 사진 공모전에서 수상한 것 축하해. 학교 강당에서 네 사진 봤는데 정말 다른 작품들보다 돋보였어. 모든 학생들이 네 작품 보려고 몰려들었는데, 대단하더라. 네가 부탁했던 역사 숙제 말인데 당연히 도와줄 수 있어. 한 시간 뒤에 공공 도서관에서 만나는 건 어때? 난 지금 바로 거기로 갈게. 그리고 노트북 꼭 가지고 와. 자료 조사하려면 필요하니까.

M: 소년이 소녀에게 만나자고 한 장소는 어디입니까?

(A) 도서관
(B) 소녀의 집
(C) 학교 강당

19.

G: Mom, you don't need to drop off my dress at the dry cleaners today. I found out that I only need it for the day of the piano concert. I thought we had to wear it for the rehearsal, but Mr. Gibson said wearing my uniform is not a problem. Oh, another thing: when I was at the mall with Amanda, I found the perfect shoes to match my dress. How about we go to the mall so I can show them to you?

M: Why did the girl call?

G: 엄마, 오늘 제 드레스 드라이클리닝 맡기지 않으셔도 돼요. 피아노 연주회 당일에만 필요하요. 리허설 때도 입어야 하는 줄 알았는데, Gibson 선생님이 교복 입어도 괜찮다고 하셨어요. 아참, 다른 얘긴데 Amanda랑 쇼핑몰에 갔다가 드레스랑 딱 어울리는 신발을 찾았어요. 엄마랑 같이 가서 보여드리면 어때요?

M: 소녀는 왜 전화했나요?

(A) 쇼핑몰에 가서 신발을 살 수 있는지 물어보기 위해
(B) 피아노 연주회 때 교복을 입을 예정이라고 엄마에게 말하기 위해
(C) 쇼핑몰에서 신발을 왜 샀는지 엄마에게 설명하기 위해

20.

B: Hi, Arthur, it's Sean. I'm really glad to hear that you've settled into your new environment. Moving can be a big change, but it's great to know you're doing well. Thank you for the pictures that you sent; they all looked great. Actually, I was thinking. As the summer holidays are around the corner, I was wondering if you'd like to come and visit. It would be great to catch up on everything.

M: What did Sean call about?

B: 여보세요, Arthur. 나 Sean이야. 새로운 환경에 잘 적응하고 있다고 하니 기뻐. 이사는 큰 변화일 수 있는데, 잘 지내고 있다니 다행이야. 보내준 사진들 고마워. 다 멋지더라. 사실 말인데, 여름 방학이 곧 다가오잖아. 너 혹시 우리 집에 놀러 올 생각 있어? 그동안 못한 얘기 나누면 좋을 것 같아.

M: Sean이 전화한 이유는 무엇입니까?

(A) Arthur에게 잘 지내고 있다고 말하기 위해

(B) Arthur가 곧 방문하도록 확인하기 위해

(C) 여름 방학을 함께 보낼 생각이 있는지 물어보기 위해

21.

W: This is Caroline calling about the coat I purchased for my son. I would like to know if I can return it since it doesn't fit him. Do you have it available in a larger size? The color really suited him, but the size did not. He needs it for his speech next week. If you don't have a larger size in stock, I would like to place an order. However, if it can't arrive by the weekend, I would prefer a refund.

M: Why did Caroline call?

W: Caroline입니다. 아들을 위해 구입한 코트에 대해 전화 드렸어요. 사이즈가 맞지 않아서 반품이 가능한지 알고 싶습니다. 혹시 더 큰 사이즈가 있나요? 색상은 아들에게 정말 잘 어울리지만, 사이즈가 안 맞아요. 다음 주 연설에 필요해서요. 혹시 더 큰 사이즈 재고가 없으면 주문하고 싶어요. 하지만 주말까지 도착하지 않으면 환불을 원합니다.

M: Caroline은 왜 전화했나요?

(A) 코트를 다른 색으로 바꾸기 위해

(B) 더 큰 사이즈의 코트를 받을 수 있는지 알아보기 위해

(C) 오늘 환불받을 수 있는지 물어보기 위해

22.

M: Good afternoon, Mr. Lee. This is Principal Jefferson. I am pleased to share some great news with you. Your son, Aaron, has received a scholarship for academic excellence this year. As you know, there will be an award ceremony next week to honor all students receiving scholarships. We invite all parents to join us, and we will be providing refreshments and light snacks. To help us finalize the arrangements, please confirm your attendance by Thursday. I hope to see you at the ceremony next Wednesday!

M: Why is Principal Jefferson calling Mr. Lee?

M: 안녕하세요, Aaron 아버님. 저는 Jefferson 교장입니다. 좋은 소식을 전해드리게 되었습니다. 선생님의 아들 Aaron이 올해 학업 우수 장학금을 받게 되었습니다. 아시다시피, 다음 주에 모든 수상 학생들을 위한 시상식이 열릴 예정입니다. 모든 학부모님들을 초대하며, 간단한 다과도 제공될 예정입니다. 행사 준비를 위해 목요일까지 참석 여부를 알려주시기 바랍니다. 다음 주 수요일 시상식에서 뵙기를 바랍니다!

M: Jefferson 교장 선생님이 Aaron 아버지에게 전화한 이유는 무엇입니까?

(A) 다음 주에 시상식이 열린다는 것을 알리기 위해

(B) 목요일에 열리는 시상식에 Aaron 아버지를 초대하기 위해

(C) Aaron 아버지가 시상식에 참여할 수 있는지 확인하기 위해

23.

W: Ria, I know you're with your dad, but he seems to be busy on the phone. Can you please let him know that he needs to pick up a few things before getting home? First, he should go pick up Grandma and take her to the mall, where she is planning to meet her friends. Also, I ordered a new suit for him, so while he's dropping Grandma off, please remind him to pick it up on the way. I know that I told him last night, but please remind him again.

M: Why did Ria's mom call?

W: Ria, 지금 아빠랑 같이 있는 거 아는데, 아빠가 통화 중인 것 같구나. 아빠한테 집에 오기 전에 몇 가지 할 일이 있다고 좀 전해줄래? 먼저, 할머니를 쇼핑몰에 모셔다 드려야 해. 거기서 할머니가 친구들을 만나실 예정이거든. 그리고 아빠 새 정장을 주문해 뒀으니까, 할머니를 모셔다드리는 김에 정장을 꼭 찾아오라고 전해주렴. 어젯밤에도 말해 놓긴 했지만, 다시 한번 꼭 상기시켜줘.

M: Ria의 엄마가 전화한 이유는 무엇입니까?

(A) 엄마가 아빠의 정장을 찾고 있다고 말해주기 위해

(B) 할머니가 쇼핑몰에서 친구들과 함께 있다고 말해주기 위해

(C) 아빠가 정장 찾는 것을 Ria에게 상기시켜 달라고 하기 위해

24.

W: Hey, Isaac, it's Coach Christina. I wanted to talk about your performance at the hockey match yesterday. I was really impressed with your concentration throughout the game, and the goals you scored were incredible. Even though it was a challenging match, you did an outstanding job. I've received a call from the tournament officials, and they informed me that you will soon receive the MVP award, meaning you're the most valuable player. How about I explain everything over lunch today? Can you come by my office around 12:30? You're the youngest student in the school's history to receive the MVP award.

M: What will Isaac do at lunch?

W: Isaac, 안녕. Christina 코치야. 어제 하키 경기에서의 네 경기력에 대해 얘기하려고 해. 경기 내내 집중하는 모습이 인상적이었고, 네가 넣은 골들도 정말 대단했어. 힘든 경기였지만 훌륭하게 해냈어. 대회 관계자에게 전화가 왔는데, 네가 곧 MVP를 받게 될거라고 알려줬고, 이는 네가 최우수 선수라는 뜻이야. 점심시간에 내가 자세히 설명해 줄게, 어때? 내 사무실로 12시 30분쯤 올 수 있겠니? 너는 학교 역사상 MVP 상을 받는 최연소 학생이야.

M: Isaac이 점심시간에 할 일은 무엇입니까?

(A) MVP 수여받기

(B) 자신이 경기를 얼마나 잘했는지 설명하기

(C) 코치 얘기 듣기

25.

G: Hello, it's Penny. Thank you so much for taking the time to agree to do this interview. I have been your number-one fan for a long time, and it feels like a dream talking to you. I have seen nearly all of your matches, and watching you play has always inspired me. Your sportsmanship and continuous skill development motivate me to follow my dreams. I want to become someone like you one day. As a final note, thank you for inviting me to your match next month. It means the world to me.

M: Why did Penny call?

G: 안녕하세요, Penny입니다. 이번 인터뷰에 응해 주셔서 정말 감사드려요. 오래전부터 선수님의 열렬한 팬이었는데, 이렇게 직접 대화를 나누는 게 꿈만 같아요. 저는 선수님이 뛰시는 거의 모든 경기를 봤고, 선수님의 플레이를 보는 것은 늘 저에게 큰 영감을 줬습니다. 선수님의 스포츠맨십과 끊임없는 실력 향상은 제가 제 꿈을 따라가도록 동기 부여가 돼요. 언젠가는 저도 선수님과 같은 사람이 되고 싶어요. 마지막으로, 다음 달 경기 초대해 주셔서 감사드립니다. 저에게는 너무나도 의미가 큰 일입니다.

M: Penny는 왜 전화했나요?

(A) 최근 경기가 최고였다고 말하기 위해

(B) 훌륭한 롤모델이 되어준 것에 감사의 뜻을 전하기 위해

(C) 다음 달 그녀의 경기에 초대장을 보냈다고 말하기 위해

Part 4.

[26-29] 다음을 듣고, 26-29번 질문에 답하세요.

W: "Wow! Look at that long roller coaster; it looks so exciting! How about we get on that one first? I think it's called the Sailing Cruise," Lucy exclaimed.

"It looks really fun; can you see how fast it's going? Oh, but look at that long line of people. I think they're all waiting to get on it," said Daisy.

"It is a long line. How about we go ice skating first? I heard that the ice rink was renovated this year, and it's gotten much bigger!" suggested Grace.

"Sounds like a plan! Let's check out the arcade zone afterward, too. The last time I was here, I had so much fun playing air hockey and the basketball hoop game," answered Lucy.

Nodding with agreement, Daisy said, "I played mini-bowling

with my sister, and I had so much fun, too!"

As the three friends were on their way to the ice rink, a delicious smell of popcorn and caramel filled the air. They all made their way to the popcorn vendor, and before they knew it, they had chosen their favorite flavors. With a bucket full of popcorn in each hand, they arrived at the ice rink.

"Can you believe how big the ice rink is? They did a great job renovating the place. Also, only a few people are here today, so we have the place to ourselves," Daisy said with enthusiasm.

While Grace and Daisy put on the ice skates, Lucy worriedly said, "I've never been ice skating before; I hope it's not too hard."

"Don't worry, we've got you. All you have to take is baby steps. It's just like rollerblading, and I know how good you are with that," said Grace in an encouraging voice.

After about 30 minutes, the three friends were having a wonderful time. It was Lucy who was having the most fun. She had natural talent and glided on the ice with great speed.

"I didn't realize how ice skating can be so fun! I'm so hungry after all that skating. Let's go get lunch!" yelled Lucy as she raced over the ice rink.

W: "와! 저 긴 롤러코스터 좀 봐! 정말 신나 보여! 저거 먼저 타는 거 어때? '세일링 크루즈'라고 부른대." Lucy가 소리쳤습니다.

"정말 재미있어 보인다. 빠른 거 보여? 아, 그런데 줄 긴 것 좀 봐. 다들 저거 타려고 기다리는 것 같아." Daisy가 말했습니다.

"줄이 길긴 하네. 그럼 아이스 스케이트 먼저 타는 건 어때? 올해 아이스링크가 리모델링돼서 훨씬 커졌다고 들었어!" Grace가 제안했습니다.

"좋은 생각이다! 그 다음엔 아케이드 존에도 가보자. 지난번에 여기 왔을 때 에어 하키랑 농구 슛 게임 진짜 재미있었거든." Lucy가 대답했습니다.

Daisy가 고개를 끄덕이며 말했습니다. "나도 동생이랑 미니 볼링 쳤는데 정말 재밌었어!"

세 친구가 아이스링크로 가는 길에 팝콘과 캐러멜의 맛있는 냄새가 공중에 가득 퍼졌습니다. 그들은 모두 팝콘 판매대로 향했고, 자신들도 모르게 각자 좋아하는 맛을 골라 들고 있었습니다. 그들은 손에 팝콘이 가득 담긴 통을 들고 아이스링크에 도착했습니다.

"아이스링크가 이렇게 크다는 거 믿어져? 리모델링 정말 잘했다. 게다가 오늘 사람이 별로 없어서 우리만 쓰는 것 같아!" Daisy가 신나서 말했습니다.

Grace와 Daisy가 스케이트를 신는 동안, Lucy가 걱정스러운 목소리로 말했습니다. "나 아이스 스케이트 한 번도 안 타봤는데, 너무 어렵지 않았으면 좋겠어."

"걱정 마, 우리가 도와줄게. 차근차근 하면 돼. 롤러블레이드랑 똑같아. 너 그거 잘 타잖아." Grace가 격려하며 말했습니다.

30분쯤 지나 세 친구는 즐거운 시간을 보내고 있었습니다. 가장 재미있어하는 사람은 Lucy였습니다. Lucy는 타고난 재능이 있었고 엄

청난 속도로 얼음 위를 미끄러져 다녔습니다.
"아이스 스케이트가 이렇게 재미있을 줄 몰랐어! 실컷 탔더니 배고프다. 점심 먹으러 가자!" Lucy가 아이스링크 위를 가로지르며 소리쳤습니다.

26. 세 친구는 롤러코스터의 긴 줄을 본 후 무엇을 했습니까?

(A) 줄을 서서 기다렸다.
(B) 아케이드 존에 가기로 했다.
(C) 아이스링크로 가기로 했다.

27. Lucy가 아케이드 존에서 해 본 게임이 <u>아닌</u> 것은 무엇입니까?

(A) 미니 볼링
(B) 농구 슛 게임
(C) 에어 하키

28. Lucy는 처음으로 아이스 스케이트를 타고 나서 어땠습니까?

(A) 걱정했다.
(B) 신이 났다.
(C) 불안했다.

29. 세 친구가 다음으로 갈 곳은 어디입니까?

(A) 아케이드 존 가기
(B) 식당 가기
(C) 세일링 크루즈

[30-33] 다음을 듣고, 30-33번 질문에 답하세요.

W: Two sisters, Sara and Sally were playing in the park with their dog, Lizzy. Lizzy was a big Labrador with fine black fur and ears shaped like triangles. They took turns throwing a ball for Lizzy, who loved to fetch. The playful dog dashed around the park, trying to catch the balls as they were thrown. Among the many games Lizzy enjoyed, such as tug-of-war, hide-and-seek, and frisbee, fetch was her absolute favorite.

While Lizzy was busy fetching, Sara went to the bench to drink some water. "I think Lizzy wants water too; she's panting quite loudly," said Sally, looking at Lizzy fondly. "I agree. Can you go and get Lizzy's water bowl? It's in Mom's car," replied Sara.

As Sally walked to the car, she wiped the sweat from her face. When she opened the trunk and found the water bowl, she noticed Lizzy, still full of energy, waiting for her to return quickly. It was mid-afternoon, and the sun was becoming increasingly hot.

Suddenly, Sally wondered how dogs cool down. "Sara, we sweat to cool off, but how does Lizzy cool down?" she asked. "Great question! Do you see how Lizzy is panting

right now? That's her primary method of cooling down. When dogs pant, cool air enters through their mouths and noses, which helps lower their body temperature. They also try to stay in cooler places, like lying on cool surfaces," explained Sara.

"Oh, that's why Lizzy is lying down in the shade! I'll go get the water bottle right now!" exclaimed Sally.

W: 자매인 Sara와 Sally가 반려견 Lizzy와 함께 공원에서 놀고 있었습니다. Lizzy는 삼각형 모양의 귀를 가진 윤기 나는 검은 털의 대형 래브라도견입니다. 그 들이 번갈아 가며 Lizzy에게 공을 던져주면 Lizzy는 신나게 공을 물어왔습니다. 장난기 많은 Lizzy는 공이 던져질 때마다 공원 곳곳을 뛰어다니며 공을 잡으려 했습니다. Lizzy는 줄다리기, 숨바꼭질, 프리스비를 포함한 여러 놀이 중에서도 공물어오기를 가장 좋아했습니다. Lizzy가 바쁘게 공을 물어 오는 동안, Sara는 벤치로 가서 물을 마셨습니다. "Lizzy도 물 마시고 싶나 봐. 헉헉거리는 소리가 크잖아." Sally가 Lizzy를 다정하게 바라보며 말했습니다. "맞아. Lizzy 물 그릇 좀 가져다줄래? 엄마 차에 있어." Sara가 대답했습니다.

Sally는 차로 걸어가면서 얼굴의 땀을 닦았습니다. 트렁크를 열고 물그릇을 찾았을 때, 여전히 에너지 넘치는 Lizzy가 자신이 빨리 돌아오기를 기다리고 있는 것을 알아차렸습니다. 한낮이었고, 해는 점점 더 뜨거워지고 있었습니다.

문득 Sally는 개들이 어떻게 더위를 식히는지 궁금해졌습니다. "Sara, 우리는 땀을 흘려서 더위를 식히잖아. 근데 Lizzy는 어떻게 더위를 식힐까?" Sally가 물었습니다. "좋은 질문이야! Lizzy가 헉헉 거리는 것 보이지? 그게 더위를 식히는 주된 방법이야. 개들이 헉헉 거리면 시원한 공기가 입과 코를 통해 들어가면서 체온을 낮추는 데 도움이 돼. 개들은 또 서늘한 바닥에 눕는 것처럼 더 시원한 곳에 머무르는 방법을 쓰기도 해." Sara가 설명했습니다.

"아, 그래서 Lizzy가 그늘에 누워 있었구나! 지금 바로 물병 가져올게!" Sally가 외쳤습니다.

30. Lizzy가 가장 좋아하는 놀이는 무엇입니까?

(A) 프리스비
(B) 공 물어오기
(C) 숨바꼭질

31. Sally가 본 Lizzy는 어떻게 보였습니까?

(A) 많이 뛰어서 피곤해 보였다.
(B) Sara가 돌아오길 기다리며 지루해하는 것처럼 보였다.
(C) 공 물어오기 놀이를 한 후에도 에너지가 넘쳐 보였다.

32. Sally가 발견한 Lizzy의 모습은 어땠습니까?

(A) 너무 신나서 헉헉거리고 있었다.
(B) 물을 마시고 싶어 하는 것처럼 보였다.
(C) 좋아하는 다른 놀이를 하고 싶어 하는 것처럼 보였다.

33. Lizzy는 몸을 식히러 어디로 갔나요?

(A) 집
(B) 엄마 차
(C) 그늘

[34-36] 다음을 듣고, 34-36번 질문에 답하세요.

M: Did you know that telescopes are among the greatest inventions people have ever created? They've been around for about 400 years, and while the early ones were made with hand-polished glass, which made them difficult to use, modern telescopes can be used by anyone and come in various sizes. Compared to early telescopes, which only scientists could use, today, anyone can use one, in schools or in their backyard! There are even giant telescopes floating on earth called radio telescopes that use huge metal dishes to receive signals from the stars. So, how do telescopes work exactly? Telescopes have two main parts. The big lens at the front, called the objective lens, gathers light and focuses it at a point. The smaller lens, known as the eyepiece, magnifies this focused light so you can see things clearly. This is how you can view distant stars and planets up close!
Isn't astronomy fascinating? Grab a telescope and start exploring the universe!

M: 사람들이 만든 발명품 중 망원경이 가장 위대한 발명품 중 하나라는 것을 알고 있었습니까? 망원경은 약 400년 동안 존재해 왔는데, 초기 망원경은 손으로 연마한 유리로 만들어져 사용하기 어려웠지만, 현대의 망원경은 누구나 사용할 수 있고 다양한 크기로 나옵니다. 과학자들만 사용할 수 있었던 초기 망원경과 비교하면, 오늘날에는 학교나 집 뒷마당에서 누구나 사용할 수 있습니다. 지구에는 별들로부터 오는 신호를 받기 위해 거대한 금속 접시를 사용하는 전파망원경이라고 불리는 초대형 망원경들도 있습니다. 그렇다면 망원경은 정확히 어떻게 작동할까요? 망원경에는 두 가지 주요 부분이 있습니다. 앞에 있는 큰 렌즈는 대물렌즈라고 불리는데, 빛을 모아서 한 지점에 초점을 맞춥니다. 작은 렌즈는 접안렌즈라고 불리며, 이 집중된 빛을 확대해서 물체를 선명하게 볼 수 있게 해 줍니다. 이렇게 해서 우리는 멀리 떨어진 별과 행성을 가까이서 관찰할 수 있는 것입니다.
천문학은 정말 흥미롭지 않습니까? 망원경을 들고 우주 탐험을 시작해 보세요.

34. 초기 망원경으로 관측하는 것이 어려웠던 이유는 무엇입니까?

(A) 유리가 손으로 연마되었기 때문에
(B) 낮에만 볼 수 있었기 때문에
(C) 과학자들만 선명하게 보는 법을 알았기 때문에

해설 과거에 제작된 망원경은 손으로 연마한 유리를 사용했기 때문에 관찰이 쉽지 않았다고 언급되었다. 이에 과학자들이 쉽게 사용할 수 있

었다는 설명은 맞지 않으며, 손으로 연마한 유리가 정답임을 뒷받침한다. 따라서 답은 (A)이다.

35. 망원경은 어떻게 작동합니까?

(A) 접안렌즈가 초점을 맞춘 빛을 확대한다.
(B) 큰 렌즈가 초점을 맞춘 빛을 확대한다.
(C) 접안렌즈가 사물을 선명하게 볼 수 있도록 도와준다.

해설 망원경의 앞부분은 objective lens로, 이는 빛을 모은 후 한 점에 초점을 맞추는 역할을 한다. 그리고 작은 렌즈인 eyepiece는 이 초점이 맞춰진 빛을 통해 사람들이 물체를 더 선명하게 볼 수 있도록 돕는다고 설명되어 있다. 보기 A에서는 eyepiece가 빛을 줄여준다고 되어 있고, B에서는 빛을 확대한다고 되어 있어 둘 다 본문의 설명과는 반대되는 내용이다. 반면 C는 eyepiece가 물체를 더 선명하게 볼 수 있게 도와준다고 했기 때문에, 본문 내용에 가장 부합하며 정답은 (C) 이다.

36. 전통적인 망원경과 전파망원경의 차이가 <u>아닌</u> 것은 무엇입니까?

(A) 크기
(B) 신호
(C) 용도

해설 과거의 망원경이 hand-polished glass로 만들어졌기 때문에 사물을 선명하게 보기 어려웠다고 설명한다. 반면, 현대의 망원경은 다양한 크기로 제작되며, 그중 거대한 망원경은 금속 반사판 (metal dishes)를 이용해 별에서 오는 신호를 포착하는 radio telescope (전파망원경) 이라고 소개된다. 이처럼 본문은 망원경의 구조와 발전 과정에 대해 설명하고 있지만, 과거 망원경이든 현대 망원경이든 공통된 목적은 '우주를 관찰하는 것' 이라는 점이 강조된다. 따라서 정답은 (C)이다.

[37-39] 다음을 듣고, 37-39번 질문에 답하세요.

W: Russia is the largest country in the world, boasting the highest number of trees and ranking as one of the largest oil producers globally. The weather has a significant impact on life in Russia. While Antarctica holds the title for the coldest place on Earth, Russia is considered the coldest country. As a result, people often stay indoors during the long, dark winter evenings.
This is one of the reasons why chess has been so popular throughout Russia, along with the rise of computer games. For instance, the classic game Tetris was invented in Russia. Despite the cold climate, Russians continue to enjoy sports. Ice hockey, ice skating, and soccer are particularly popular among the population.
An interesting fact: during the 1990s, Russia decided that students no longer needed to wear school uniforms, as they required warmer clothing. Now, children can even wear fur coats to school!

Finally, considering the vast land and cold temperatures, Russia is the world's largest producer of potatoes and barley.

W: 러시아는 세계에서 가장 큰 나라로, 나무의 수가 가장 많고 세계 최대 산유국 중 하나입니다. 날씨는 러시아의 생활에 큰 영향을 미칩니다. 남극이 지구상에서 가장 추운 곳임에도, 러시아는 가장 추운 나라로 여겨집니다. 그 결과, 사람들은 길고 어두운 겨울 저녁 동안 주로 실내에 머무릅니다.

이것이 러시아에서 체스가 오랫동안 인기를 얻었던 이유 중 하나입니다. 컴퓨터 게임의 등장도 마찬가지입니다. 예를 들어, 고전 게임인 테트리스도 러시아에서 발명되었습니다. 추운 기후에도 불구하고, 러시아인들은 계속해서 스포츠를 즐깁니다. 특히, 아이스하키, 아이스 스케이팅, 축구가 인기가 많습니다.

흥미로운 사실 하나 알려 드리죠. 러시아는 1990년대에 학생들이 더 따뜻한 옷을 입을 수 있도록 교복 착용을 의무화하지 않기로 결정했습니다. 지금 학생들은 심지어 모피 코트를 입고 학교에 갈 수도 있습니다!

마지막으로, 넓은 국토와 추운 기온 덕분에 러시아는 세계 최대의 감자와 보리 생산국입니다.

37. 선생님이 이야기하고 있는 것은 무엇입니까?

(A) 러시아의 유명한 발명품
(B) 날씨가 러시아에 미치는 영향
(C) 러시아가 생산하는 음식의 종류

38. 요즘 러시아에서 컴퓨터 게임이 인기 있는 이유는 무엇입니까?

(A) 대부분의 컴퓨터 게임이 러시아에서 발명되었기 때문에
(B) 체스보다 더 재미있기 때문에
(C) 실내에서 즐기기 좋은 게임이기 때문에

39. 선생님이 남극을 언급한 이유는 무엇입니까?

(A) 남극의 크기와 러시아를 비교하기 위해
(B) 러시아가 얼마나 추운지 설명하기 위해
(C) 남극에 대한 흥미로운 사실을 말하기 위해

Reading

1	(B)	**2**	(A)	**3**	(C)	**4**	(C)
5	(C)	**6**	(C)	**7**	(B)	**8**	(B)
9	(B)	**10**	(A)	**11**	(A)	**12**	(C)
13	(B)	**14**	(A)	**15**	(C)	**16**	(B)
17	(A)	**18**	(C)	**19**	(B)	**20**	(C)
21	(B)	**22**	(A)	**23**	(A)	**24**	(C)
25	(A)	**26**	(C)	**27**	(B)	**28**	(A)
29	(C)	**30**	(B)	**31**	(C)	**32**	(A)
33	(C)	**34**	(B)	**35**	(C)	**36**	(B)
37	(C)						

Part 1.

1. 이것은 몸의 일부입니다. 이것은 손에 있습니다. 이것은 열 개 중 하나입니다. 이것은 무엇입니까?

(A) 발가락
(B) 손가락
(C) 발

2. 생일 파티에 8명이 옵니다. 테이블 위에 접시는 8개 있지만, 포크와 유리잔은 7개씩밖에 없습니다. 포크가 _____ 때문에 다시 찬장으로 갑니다.

(A) 충분하지 않다
(B) 충분하다
(C) 너무 많다

3. 어떤 아이들은 숨바꼭질을 하고 있습니다. 어떤 아이들은 그네를 탑니다. 아이들이 놀 수 있는 다양한 활동들이 있습니다. 아이들이 있는 곳은 _____입니다.

(A) 수영장
(B) 도서관
(C) 놀이터

4. 영화관에 가려고 합니다. 버스를 탔는데, 사람이 너무 많습니다. 많은 사람이 서로 가까이 붙어서 서 있습니다. 이 버스는 _____.

(A) 공간이 넓다
(B) 면적이 넓다
(C) 혼잡하다

5. 그는 휴대전화를 들고 있었습니다. 메시지가 하나 왔지만, 누가 보낸 것인지 몰랐습니다. 스팸 메시지 같아서 메시지를 지웠습니다. 그는 어떤 행동을 했습니까?

(A) 메시지를 열어 보았다
(B) 휴대전화를 충전했다
(C) 메시지를 삭제했다

6. 이 개는 매우 활동적입니다. 하루에 세 번 산책을 나갑니다. 쉬지도 않고 하루 종일 놀고 싶어 합니다. 이 개는 _____.

(A) 깡충깡충 뛰는 중이다
(B) 흔들리는 중이다
(C) 힘이 넘친다

7. 우리 반은 다른 반과 축구 경기를 했습니다. 전반전 점수는 1대 1이었습니다. 경기 종료 휘슬이 울리기 10초 전, 우리 팀이 골을 넣었습니다. 우리는 상대 팀을 상대로 _____.

(A) 지다
(B) 이기다
(C) 내기를 하다

8. 여름이고, 날씨가 매우 덥습니다. 많은 사람들이 더운 날씨에 이 것들을 발에 착용합니다. 이것을 신으면 발이 시원합니다. 이것은 _____입니다.

(A) 목걸이
(B) 샌들
(C) 수영복

9. 영어 선생님이 모르는 단어를 말씀하십니다. 수업이 곧 끝나려고 합니다. 수업이 끝나고 당신은 이 단어를 _____.

(A) 보다
(B) 찾다
(C) 훑어보다

10. 그는 가게 안에 있습니다. 과일 봉지를 손님에게 건네어주고 있습니다. 그는 여성에게 5달러를 받고 거스름돈을 줍니다. 그는 무엇을 하고 있습니까?

(A) 과일 판매
(B) 과일 구매
(C) 과일 수확

11. 한 소녀가 댄스 공연을 보고 있습니다. 댄서들은 팔과 다리를 다양한 방식으로 움직이고 있습니다. 소녀는 일어나서 그 동작들을 따라 해 보려 합니다. 소녀는 춤 동작을 _____ 있습니다.

(A) 흉내 내다
(B) 접다
(C) 들다

Part 2.

[12-15] 아래를 읽고, 12–15번 질문에 답하세요.

지역 소방서 견학

5학년 학생들에게 알립니다!

이번 주 수요일, 지역 소방서로 견학을 갑니다. 안전 교육을 배우고 소방관의 중요한 역할을 이해할 수 있는 좋은 기회입니다. 모든 학생은 견학 후 이번 방문에 대해 짧은 글을 써야 합니다. 가장 좋았던 부분과 배운 점을 꼭 포함해야 합니다.

수요일 일정

오전 10:00	소방서 도착
오전 10:30 – 오전 11:30	소방서 투어
오전 11:30 – 오후 1:00	화재 안전 수업
오후 1:00 – 오후 2:00	점심 식사
오후 2:00 – 오후 2:30	단체 사진 촬영
오후 2:30	학교 복귀

기타 안내
– 소방관의 말을 적을 수 있도록 공책과 연필을 준비하세요.
– 편한 옷과 신발을 착용하세요.
– 도시락을 준비해 오세요.

---

12. 학생들이 지역 소방서에 가는 이유는 무엇입니까?

(A) 화재 안전 포스터를 만들기 위해
(B) 소방관을 인터뷰하기 위해
(C) 안전 교육을 받기 위해

13. 학생들이 소방서 투어를 하는 시간은 몇 시입니까?

(A) 오전 10:00
(B) 오전 10:30
(C) 오전 11:00

14. 학생들이 글에 포함하지 <u>않아도</u> 되는 것은 무엇입니까?

(A) 가장 좋았던 소방관
(B) 가장 인상 깊었던 부분
(C) 배운 내용

15. 화재 안전 수업 시간은 얼마나 걸립니까?

(A) 30분
(B) 1시간
(C) 1시간 30분

안녕하세요, 할머니!

아빠가 말씀드렸나요? 저 과학 전시회에서 1등 했어요!
그래서 국내에 있는 어떤 박물관이든 하나를 선택해서 갈 수 있게 되었어요. 그런데 어디를 갈지 아직 못 정했어요. 저 할머니처럼 애니메이션, 기차, 로봇 좋아하잖아요. 티켓이 두 장이라, 할머니를 제가 선택한 곳으로 모시고 싶어요. 좀 조사해 봤는데, 'Comuseum'은 하루 패스 하나로 모든 그래픽, 만화 전시회, 기술 관련 행사를 관람할 수 있고, 경품도 받을 수 있어요(저 공짜 선물 좋아하는 것 아시죠?) 그리고 'M.O.T.(기술 박물관)'도 찾아봤어요. 여기 하루 패스로는 놀이 기구, 멋진 전시와 발명품들을 즐길 수 있지만 경품은 없어요. 어디로 가는 것이 좋을까요?

사랑을 담아,
Grace 드림

16. Grace가 받는 상품에 대한 사실이 <u>아닌</u> 것은 무엇입니까?

(A) 국내 박물관에 갈 수 있다.
(B) 해외 박물관에 갈 수 있다.
(C) 도시 내의 박물관에 갈 수 있다.

17. Grace는 할머니가 어떤 박물관을 선택하길 가장 바랄까요?

(A) 경품을 주는 박물관
(B) 놀이기구가 있는 박물관
(C) 발명품들이 있는 박물관

받는 사람: Violet, Ria
보낸 사람: Sophia
제목: 파자마 파티

내일 파자마 파티 너무 기대돼! 모두 어떤 파자마 입을지 정했어? 나는 내가 제일 좋아하는 파란색 파자마로 골랐어. 진짜 포근하고 따뜻해. 좋아하는 인형도 꼭 챙겨와! 우리 진짜 재밌게 놀자!
엄마랑 나는 간식이랑 핫초코 사러 시장에 갈 거야. 혹시 먹고 싶은 간식 있어? 그럼 전화해서 알려줘! 같이 볼 영화도 하나 골라놨는데, 혹시 보고 싶은 영화가 있으면 가져와도 돼! 보드게임은 내가 많이 준비해 뒀으니까 따로 안 챙겨와도 괜찮아.

모두 곧 만나.

사랑을 담아,
Sophia

18. Sophia와 엄마는 왜 시장에 갑니까?

(A) 영화를 빌리기 위해
(B) 파자마를 사기 위해
(C) 간식을 사기 위해

19. Sophia와 친구들이 하게 될 일이 <u>아닌</u> 것은 무엇입니까?

(A) 보드게임을 한다.
(B) 책을 읽는다.
(C) 영화를 본다.

보물찾기!

오늘은 친구들과 함께 팀을 이루어 팀워크를 보여줄 시간입니다. 여러분의 임무는 아래 목록에 있는 물건들을 찾는 것이고, 정해진 시간 안에 가장 많은 물건을 찾는 팀이 상품을 받게 됩니다. 모든 물건을 찾으면 목록에 체크하고 선생님께 가져오세요.

보물찾기 목록
– 바퀴 달린 물건
– 나무로 만들어진 물건
– 반짝이는 물건
– 부드러운 물건
– Y자 모양의 나뭇가지
– 클로버
– 솔방울
– 빨간 꽃

모든 물건은 운동장, 정원, 도서관 등 학교 교내에서 찾을 수 있습니다. 하지만 주차장에는 많은 차들이 드나들기 때문에 가지 마세요. 또한, 정보를 공유하고 서로 소통하며 팀워크를 발휘하는 것을 잊지 마세요. 제한 시간은 30분이며, 만약 한 팀도 끝내지 못할 경우에는 30분이 추가로 주어집니다.

** 위험해 보이는 것은 줍거나 만지지 마세요! 목록에 있는 안전한 것만 모아야 합니다.

20. 모든 물건을 다 모은 후에는 무엇을 해야 합니까?

(A) 사진을 찍는다.
(B) 집에 가져간다.
(C) 선생님께 가져간다.

21. 물건들은 어디에서 찾아야 합니까?

(A) 지역 도서관
(B) 놀이터
(C) 주차장

22. 30분 안에 한 팀도 끝내지 못하면 얼마나 추가로 주어집니까?

(A) 30분
(B) 1시간
(C) 1시간 30분

[23-25] 다음을 읽고, 23-25번 질문에 답하세요.

원더랜드 공항

처음으로 공항에 가서 비행기를 타는 것은 누구에게나 매우 신나는 일입니다. 즐거운 여행이 될 수 있도록, 아래의 사항들을 확인해 계획이 차질없이 진행되도록 해보세요.

공항에 가기 전
✓ 티켓 확인하기: 전자 항공권 또는 종이 항공권
✓ 짐 싸기
✓ 여권 챙겼는지 확인
✓ 항공편 출발 최소 2시간 전에 출발하기

공항에서
1. 체크인 카운터: 수하물을 체크인 데스크에 맡기세요.
2. 보안 검색대: 항공사 직원에게 여권을 보여주세요.
3. 탑승 전, 전광판에서 탑승 게이트와 항공편 번호를 확인하세요.
4. 탑승:
  – 줄을 서서 승무원에게 항공권을 보여주세요.
  – 비행기에 탑승하세요.
  – 좌석에 앉아 안전벨트를 매세요.
5. 비행 중: 창밖을 보며 아름다운 풍경을 즐겨보세요.
6. 착륙: 비행기에서 내리기 전에 소지품을 모두 챙겼는지 확인하세요.
7. 수하물 찾기: 안내 표지판을 따라가 수하물을 찾으세요.

** 항상 여권을 소지하세요.
** 시간을 항상 확인하세요.

---

23. 공항에 몇 시간 전에 출발하면 안되나요?

(A) 1시간 전
(B) 2시간 전
(C) 3시간 전

24. 보안 검색대에서는 무엇을 합니까?

(A) 수하물을 확인한다.
(B) 항공권을 보여준다.
(C) 여권을 보여준다.

25. 비행기에서 내리기 전에 무엇을 확인해야 합니까?

(A) 모든 소지품을 챙겼는지
(B) 안전벨트를 매었는지
(C) 창밖의 아름다운 풍경을 봤는지

[26-29] 다음을 읽고, 26-29번 질문에 답하세요.

11월, 여느 때처럼 Jordan과 그의 가족은 매년 먹는 추수감사절 저녁 식사를 준비하느라 바빴습니다. 온 집안에 맛있는 음식 냄새가 가득했고, 가족들은 식탁에 둘러앉을 준비를 하고 있었습니다.

"Jordan, 냅킨 놓는 것 좀 도와줄래? 네 여동생은 어디 있니? 접시를 놓고 있는 줄 알았는데." Jordan의 엄마가 물었습니다. "Bella가 할아버지께 드디어 자전거를 탈 수 있다는 걸 보여드리려고, 지금 할아버지와 함께 정원에 있어요! 냅킨이랑 접시는 이미 식탁에 올려놓았어

요." Jordan이 대답했습니다. "고마워! 넌 항상 큰 도움이 되는구나! 이제 저녁 준비가 거의 다 됐으니, 가족들에게 식탁에 둘러앉으라고 해줄래?" Jordan의 엄마가 커다란 구운 칠면조를 들고 오며 말했습니다.

10분이 되지 않아, Jordan의 가족들은 식탁에 둘러앉아 식사할 준비를 하고 있었습니다. 식탁 위에는 칠면조, 크랜베리 소스, 으깬 감자, 그레이비소스, 고구마 캐서롤, 호박파이 등 맛있는 음식들이 가득했습니다.

"이 근사한 식사를 하기 전에, 돌아가면서 감사한 것들을 말해볼까?" Jordan의 아빠가 말했습니다.
Bella가 신이 나서 손을 들었습니다. "저는 먼저 아빠에게 감사드리고 싶어요. 자전거 타는 법 가르쳐 주셔서요. 처음에는 어려웠는데 아빠가 인내심을 가지고 가르쳐 주셨어요. 감사해요."
"네가 열심히 노력한 것이 자랑스럽구나, Bella 네가 열심히 한 덕분이야, 정말 잘했어! Jordan, 너는 어떠니?" Jordan의 아빠가 물었습니다.
"저는 할아버지, 할머니께서 항상 제 곁에 있어주신 것에 감사 드려요. 최선을 다하고 사람들에게 친절하고 정직하게 대하는 것이 중요하다는 것을 가르쳐 주셨어요. 또, 할아버지 할머니의 격려는 제게 정말 큰 힘이 되었어요. 항상 말씀해주신 것을 생각하며 최선을 다할게요." Jordan이 대답했습니다.

Jordan의 아버지는 자랑스러운 듯 환하게 웃으며 말했습니다. "할아버지 할머니께 그런 좋은 말씀을 드려줘서 고맙다. 정말 자랑스럽구나. 제가 감사하게 여기는 것은 이 맛있는 식사입니다! 이렇게 훌륭한 저녁을 준비해 주신 Jordan 엄마와 어머니께 감사한다는 말을 하고 싶습니다."

26. 이 이야기는 무엇에 관한 것입니까?

(A) 요리 솜씨가 좋은 Jordan의 엄마에게 감사하는 것
(B) 서로 맛있는 음식을 만들어 준 것에 대해 감사하는 것
(C) 서로가 해준 일들에 대해 감사하는 것

27. 엄마는 왜 Jordan에게 고마워했습니까?

(A) 좋은 오빠로서 여동생에게 자전거 타는 법을 가르쳐줘서
(B) 좋은 아들로서 엄마를 도와줘서
(C) 좋은 아들로서 요리를 도와줘서

28. Jordan의 가족이 식탁에 앉은 후 바로 식사를 시작하지 않은 이유는 무엇입니까?

(A) 서로에게 감사 인사를 나누기 위해
(B) 더 많은 가족들이 도착하길 기다리기 위해
(C) 음식이 다 익기를 기다리기 위해

29. Jordan은 앞으로 어떻게 행동할 것입니까?

(A) 하고 싶은 대로 할 것이다.
(B) 자전거 타는 연습을 열심히 할 것이다.
(C) 다른 사람들을 친절히 대하고 존중할 것이다.

[30-33] 다음을 읽고, 30-33번 질문에 답하세요.

> "아빠, 너무 피곤한데 잠이 안 와요. 오후에는 졸렸는데, 지금 자정인데 정신이 말똥말똥해요." Meredith가 큰 소리로 말했습니다. "시차를 겪는 건 정상이야, Meredith. 비행기로 다른 시간대로 이동한 다음에는 많은 사람들이 이런 일을 겪어." 아빠가 대답했습니다.
> "다른 시간대요? 전에 들어본 것 같은데, 정확히 뭐예요?" Meredith가 물었습니다. "좋은 질문이야! 지구가 한 바퀴 완전히 도는 데 24시간이 걸리기 때문에, 전 세계에는 24개의 주요 시간대가 있단다. 위도와 경도의 차이를 기억하니?" Meredith의 아빠가 물었습니다. "기억해요! 위도는 수평으로, 동서로 뻗어 있고, 경도는 수직으로, 남북으로 뻗어 있어요. 본초 자오선도 알아요. 경도 0도선이 북극에서 남극까지 이어지잖아요. 이 선이 지구를 동반구와 서반구로 나눈다는 것을 배웠어요." Meredith가 신나서 대답했습니다.
> "정말 자랑스럽구나! 지리 시간에 정말 집중했네! UTC(협정 세계시)라는 것도 있어. 본초 자오선을 기준으로 하는 시간 표준으로, 다른 시간대의 시작점으로 사용돼. 전 세계 국가들이 시간을 계산할 때 기준으로 사용해." 아빠가 설명했습니다.
> "와! 그럼 UTC가 세계 시간의 기준이 되는 거군요. 그런데 사람들이 시차를 어떻게 계산하는지는 아직 설명 안 해주셨어요." Meredith가 대답했습니다.
> "이렇게 생각해 봐. 24개의 주요 시간대가 있고, 대략 1시간 간격이야. 본초 자오선에서 동쪽으로 갈수록 시간이 빨라지고, 서쪽으로 갈수록 시간이 느려져." 아빠가 설명했습니다. "그래서 어제 파리에 도착했을 때 아직 오후였던 거군요! UTC가 없으면 사람들이 정말 혼란스러울 것 같아요." Meredith가 외쳤습니다.
> "맞아! 시간이 얼마나 중요한지 네가 알아서 기쁘구나. 시간은 사람들이 전 세계를 여행하고, 일하고, 다른 사람들과 소통하는 데 도움을 준단다." Meredith의 아빠는 잠자리에 들면서 설명해 주었습니다.

30. 지구를 동반구와 서반구로 나누는 것은 무엇입니까?

(A) 협정 세계시
(B) 본초 자오선
(C) 서로 다른 시간대

해설 본초 자오선(prime meridian)이 경도 0도이며, 북극에서 남극까지 이어진다고 설명했고, 지구를 동반구와 서반구로 나누는 기준이 된다고 직접 언급되어 있다. 따라서 지구를 동서로 나눈다는 (B)가 정답이다.

31. 본문에 언급되지 <u>않은</u> 예시는 무엇입니까?

(A) 서쪽으로 이동할수록 시간이 느려진다.
(B) 지구가 한 바퀴 도는 데는 24시간이 걸린다.
(C) 경도선은 동서 방향으로 뻗어 있다.

해설 위도(latitude)는 가로 방향으로, 즉 동쪽에서 서쪽으로 이어지고, 경도(longitude)는 세로 방향, 즉 북쪽에서 남쪽으로 이어진다고 설명하고 있다. 따라서 정답은 (C)이다.

32. 주요 시간대는 서로 몇 시간 차이가 납니까?

(A) 1시간
(B) 2시간
(C) 3시간

해설 UTC(Coordinated Universal Time)가 전 세계의 표준 시간으로 사용되며, 사람들이 이 기준을 바탕으로 시간 차이를 계산하고 있다고 설명하고 있다. 또한 24개의 주요 시간대가 존재하며, 각 시간대는 보통 1시간씩 차이가 난다고 되어 있다. 이 외에도, 동쪽으로 이동할수록 시간이 1시간씩 빨라지고, 서쪽으로 갈수록 1시간씩 늦어진다는 내용도 명시되어 있다. 이러한 설명에 기반할 때, 보기 (A)가 정답이다.

33. UTC는 무엇입니까?

(A) 지구를 위도와 경도로 나누는 기준이다.
(B) 사람들이 시차를 겪도록 하는 것이다.
(C) 사람들이 시간을 맞출 때 사용하는 기준이다.

[34-35] 다음을 읽고, 34-35번 질문에 답하세요.

> 벌은 매력적인 생명체이며, 지구와 사람들에게 중요합니다. 벌의 종류는 여왕벌, 일벌, 수벌 세 가지가 있습니다. 이들은 모두 벌집이라는 큰 집에서 삽니다. 이들은 각각 다른 일을 하며 서로 협력합니다. 여왕벌은 벌 무리에서 가장 중요한 구성원입니다. 알을 낳을 수 있는 유일한 암컷 벌입니다. 일벌 또한 암컷이며, 벌 무리의 대부분을 차지합니다. 이들은 대부분의 일을 하며, 일벌 덕분에 벌들은 벌집의 조직을 유지할 수 있습니다. 일벌은 먼저 꽃에서 화밀을 모아 꿀을 만듭니다. 달콤한 화밀을 빨아들인 후, 꿀주머니에 넣습니다. 그리고 벌집으로 돌아와 화밀을 다른 벌에게 전달합니다. 그 화밀이 침 속의 특수 효소와 섞이면 꿀로 변합니다. 그런 다음, 밀랍으로 만들어진 벌집의 방에 꿀을 저장합니다. 수벌도 있습니다. 수벌은 모두 수컷이며 일벌보다 크지만 여왕벌보다는 작습니다. 수벌의 임무는 여왕벌과 짝짓기하여 더 많은 벌을 만드는 것입니다.

34. 여왕벌이 벌 무리에서 가장 중요한 구성원인 이유는 무엇입니까?

(A) 꿀을 만드는 유일한 벌이기 때문에
(B) 알을 낳을 수 있는 유일한 벌이기 때문에
(C) 벌집을 만들 수 있는 유일한 벌이기 때문에

해설 Queen Bee는 벌집에서 가장 중요한 구성원이며, 알을 낳을 수 있는 유일한 번식 암컷이라고 설명하고 있으므로, 선택지 (B)가 정답이다.

35. 수컷인 벌의 종류는 무엇입니까?

(A) 여왕벌
(B) 일벌
(C) 수벌

[36-37] 다음을 읽고, 36-37번 질문에 답하세요.

> 'B행성은 없습니다.' 사람들이 지구를 너무 많이 오염시킴에 따라 많은 환경 문제에 대한 주요 심각한 우려가 있습니다. 해수면이 상승하고, 빙하가 녹고 있으며, 멸종 위기에 처한 동물이 늘어나고 있으며, 지표면 온도도 상승하고 있습니다. 이미 벌어진 일을 되돌릴 수는 없지만, 다음 세대를 위해 지구를 구하고 더 깨끗한 곳으로 만들기 위해 함께 노력해야 합니다. 사람들이 일상생활에서 할 수 있는 간단한 행

동들이 미래에 <u>상당한</u> 변화를 가져올 것입니다. 예를 들어, 환경은 우리에게 신선한 물을 제공합니다. 우리는 이 물을 아끼고 오염시키지 않도록 주의해야 합니다. 전등을 꺼서 전기를 절약하고, 수도꼭지를 잠가 물을 절약하며, 대중교통을 이용하는 것은 이산화탄소 수치를 줄이는 데 도움이 될 것입니다. 우리가 할 수 있고 해야 하는 작은 행동들이 우리의 미래에 큰 변화를 불러올 것입니다.

36. 6번째 줄의 '상당한'의 의미는 무엇입니까?

(A) 약간의

(B) 큰

(C) 작은

37. 지구에서 일어나고 있는 문제가 <u>아닌</u> 것은 무엇입니까?

(A) 빙하가 녹고 있다.

(B) 더 많은 동물이 위기에 처해 있다.

(C) 지표면 온도가 내려가고 있다.

Listening

1 (C)	**2** (C)	**3** (C)	**4** (B)
5 (B)	**6** (C)	**7** (B)	**8** (A)
9 (A)	**10** (A)	**11** (C)	**12** (B)
13 (A)	**14** (B)	**15** (C)	**16** (C)
17 (A)	**18** (B)	**19** (A)	**20** (B)
21 (A)	**22** (B)	**23** (C)	**24** (C)
25 (B)	**26** (B)	**27** (C)	**28** (B)
29 (A)	**30** (A)	**31** (C)	**32** (B)
33 (C)	**34** (A)	**35** (C)	**36** (B)
37 (C)	**38** (C)	**39** (A)	

Part 1.

1.
W: Listen to a girl.

G: I can't believe it's already Sunday and we haven't finished all our homework. We also have a big test at school tomorrow. How about we go to our room and start preparing for it?

W: What did the girl tell her brother to do?

W: 소녀가 하는 얘기를 들어보세요.

G: 벌써 일요일이라니 믿을 수 없어. 아직 숙제도 못 끝냈는데. 내일은 학교에서 큰 시험도 있고. 우리 방에 가서 시험 준비 시작하는 게 어때?

W: 소녀는 남동생에게 무엇을 하자고 말했습니까?

2.
W: Listen to a teacher.

M: It's important to recycle what we've used instead of wasting it, and to reuse what we can. Now, we will go around the school and start putting up the posters that we've made.

W: What did the teacher tell the students to do?

W: 선생님이 하는 얘기를 들어보세요.

M: 우리가 사용한 것을 낭비하는 대신, 사용한 것을 재활용하고 가능한 것은 재사용하는 것이 중요합니다. 이제 학교 주변을 돌면서 우리가 만든 포스터를 붙이기 시작할 것입니다.

W: 선생님은 학생들에게 무엇을 하라고 말했습니까?

3.
W: Listen to a father.

M: Sally, it's important to have yearly checkups. It can help you keep a record of your health and catch any health issues you may have. Are you ready to go in?

W: What did the father ask his daughter to do?

W: 아빠가 하는 얘기를 들어보세요.

M: Sally, 매년 건강 검진을 받는 건 중요하단다. 그렇게 하면 건강 상태를 기록할 수 있고, 문제가 생기기 전에 알아챌 수 있어. 준비 됐니? 이제 들어갈까?

W: 아빠는 딸에게 무엇을 하자고 했습니까?

4.
W: Listen to a boy.

B: Why don't we go to see a play instead of the going to the movies? Watching movies is fun, but seeing the same story in musicals is even better. When you see the characters singing and dancing on stage, you're experiencing something special. The live music and atmosphere are exciting, and the audience's energy seems to grow.

W: What did the boy ask his friend to do?

W: 소년이 하는 얘기를 들어보세요.

B: 오늘 밤에 영화 말고 공연을 보는게 어때? 영화 보는 것도 재미있지만, 같은 이야기를 뮤지컬로 보는 게 훨씬 더 좋아. 무대에서 등장인물들이 노래하고 춤추는 걸 보는 건 정말 특별한 경험이야. 라이브 음악과 분위기도 신나고, 관객들의 에너지도 점점 커지는 것 같아.

W: 소년은 친구에게 무엇을 하자고 했나요?

5.
W: Listen to a teacher.

M: Steve, how about you read more nonfiction books? It's just as fun as reading comic books. It will help you think more deeply about things happening around you. It will also strengthen your thinking skills and your ways of understanding different perspectives. I can recommend a few books for you!

W: What did the teacher tell the boy to do?

W: 선생님이 하는 얘기를 들어보세요.

M: Steve, 논픽션 책을 더 읽어보는 게 어때? 만화책만큼 재미있을 수 있단다. 주변에서 일어나는 일들에 대해 더 깊이 생각하는 데 도움이 될 거야. 또한 사고력과 다양한 관점을 이해하는 능력도 키워줄 거야. 내가 몇 권 추천해 줄게.

W: 선생님은 소년에게 무엇을 하라고 말했습니까?

6.

W: Listen to a teacher.

M: Getting a good night's sleep is important for everyone. After a busy day, your body needs to rest for the next day. Sleep helps people to recover, recharge, and reset. Although our brains stay active, they are busy sorting out memories and information. Sleep is also crucial, as it helps you to feel refreshed and full of energy in the morning.

W: What did the teacher tell his students to do?

W: 선생님이 하는 얘기를 들어보세요.

M: 푹 자는 것은 모든 사람에게 중요합니다. 바쁜 하루를 보낸 뒤에는 다음 날을 위해 몸이 휴식을 취해야 합니다. 잠은 우리가 회복하고, 충전하며, 다시 시작할 수 있도록 도와줍니다. 뇌는 잠자는 동안에도 활발하지만, 기억과 정보를 정리하느라 바쁘게 움직입니다. 수면은 또한 아침에 상쾌하고 에너지로 가득 찬 기분을 느끼는 데도 중요합니다.

W: 선생님은 학생들에게 무엇을 하라고 말했습니까?

Part 2.

7.

M: Listen to a conversation between a boy and a store clerk. Listen for the answer to this question.

W: Hello! How can I help you?

B: I am looking for some flour. Where can I find it?

W: It's just over there, next to the sugar and salt.

B: Thanks. Oh, I see it.

W: Wow! That's a lot of flour. Why do you need so much?

B: I'm making a model building for a social studies project. I want it to be the biggest model in the school.

W: I think you can make a really big model building. Good luck!

B: Thank you.

M: What is the boy buying?

M: 소년과 가게 점원 사이의 대화를 듣고 질문에 답하세요.

W: 안녕하세요. 무엇을 도와드릴까요?

B: 밀가루를 찾고 있어요. 어디에 있나요?

W: 저쪽 설탕이랑 소금 옆에 있어요.

B: 감사합니다. 아, 보이네요.

W: 밀가루를 많이 사시네요. 왜 그렇게 많이 필요하세요?

B: 사회 수업 프로젝트로 건물 모형을 만들고 있어요. 학교에서 제일 큰 모형으로 만들고 싶어요.

W: 정말 큰 건물 모형을 만들 수 있겠네요. 행운을 빌어요.

B: 감사합니다.

M: 소년은 무엇을 사고 있습니까?

(A) 건물 모형을 위한 꽃

(B) 모형을 만들기 위한 밀가루

(C) 전시회를 위한 꽃, 설탕, 소금

8.

M: Listen to a conversation between a father and his daughter. Listen for the answer to this question.

G: Dad, can I help you wash your car? I had so much fun last time.

M: Of course, how about you start hosing down the car with water?

G: OK, but soaping it is my favorite.

M: Mine too! But don't forget to start from the top and make your way down.

G: I can't reach the top. Can you start first?

M: How about using that stool over there by the garage? Then you can reach the top of the car.

G: That sounds like a good idea! I'm ready!

M: Why does the girl need help washing the top of the car?

M: 아빠와 딸 사이의 대화를 듣고 질문에 답하세요.

G: 아빠, 세차 도와드릴까요? 지난번에 재밌었어요.

M: 물론이지. 먼저 차에 물 뿌리는 것부터 해볼래?

G: 네, 그런데 저는 거품 내는 게 제일 좋아요.

M: 나도 그렇단다. 하지만 위에서 시작해서 아래로 내려가는 거 잊지 마.

G: 저 위까지는 손이 안 닿아요. 아빠가 먼저 해 주실 수 있어요?

M: 차고 옆에 있는 저 의자 써보는 건 어때? 그러면 차 꼭대기도 닿을 수 있을 거야.

G: 그거 좋은 생각이예요! 준비됐어요!

M: 딸이 차 위쪽을 세차하는 데 도움이 필요했던 이유는 무엇입니까?

(A) 소녀는 키가 충분하지 않다.

(B) 소녀는 아빠가 어떻게 하는지 먼저 보고 싶어한다.

(C) 소녀는 물로 세차하는 것을 좋아하지 않는다.

9.

M: Listen to a conversation between a mother and her son. Listen for the answer to this question.

B: Mom, I have to plant some tomatoes for science class. The teacher wants us all to bring our tomatoes in two months.

W: What an interesting assignment!

B: Yes, we learned about photosynthesis at school and how plants grow, but I have no idea how to harvest them.

W: Let me help. It's not that difficult. First, why don't we go to the market to buy seeds and a pot?

B: We don't need to buy a pot; the teacher gave us each a large one. What's next?

W: If that's the case, after we return from the market, how about we find a warm spot for the tomatoes to get plenty of sunlight?

M: What will the boy and his mother do next?

M: 엄마와 아들 사이의 대화를 듣고 질문에 답하세요.

B: 엄마, 과학 수업 때문에 토마토를 심어야 해요. 선생님이 두 달 뒤에 토마토를 가져오라고 하셨어요.

W: 재밌는 과제구나!

B: 학교에서 광합성이랑 식물이 자라는 법에 대해 배웠지만, 토마토를 어떻게 수확하는지 잘 모르겠어요.

W: 내가 도와줄게. 그렇게 어렵지 않아. 먼저 시장에 가서 씨앗이랑 큰 화분을 사 올래?

B: 화분은 안 사도 돼요. 선생님께서 모두에게 큰 화분을 주셨거든요. 그다음에는요?

W: 그렇다면 시장에서 돌아온 다음, 토마토가 햇볕을 잘 받을 수 있도록 따뜻한 자리를 찾아보자.

M: 아들과 엄마는 다음에 무엇을 할 예정입니까?

(A) 시장에 가서 씨앗을 산다.
(B) 시장에 가서 커다란 화분을 산다.
(C) 토마토를 놓을 햇볕 잘 드는 자리를 찾는다.

10.

M: Listen to a conversation between a mother and her daughter. Listen for the answer to this question.

W: Sophia, what did I tell you about finishing dinner?

G: I ate everything, Mom. I've only left a few vegetables.

W: I want you to finish everything on the plate, including your greens.

G: I don't know why I have to eat them. They taste terrible.

W: Vegetables are full of nutrients to help you stay healthy. They help your body grow strong and prevent you from getting sick.

G: I wish they tasted better, like chocolate or pizza.

W: They can taste just as delicious, Sophia, try them.

G: All right, but can I have a treat afterward? Maybe cheesecake or marshmallows?

M: What will the girl probably do next?

M: 엄마와 딸 사이의 대화를 듣고 질문에 답하세요.

W: Sophia, 내가 저녁 다 먹는 것에 대해 뭐라고 말했니?
G: 다 먹었어요, 엄마. 야채만 조금 남긴 거예요.
W: 접시 위에 있는 건 다 먹어야지. 채소도 포함해서 말이야.
G: 왜 꼭 먹어야 하죠? 맛없단 말이에요.
W: 채소에는 건강하게 지낼 수 있도록 해주는 영양소가 가득한단다. 몸을 튼튼하게 자라게 하고 병에 걸리는 것을 막아주고.

G: 채소도 초콜릿이나 피자처럼 맛있었으면 좋겠어요.
W: Sophia, 채소도 충분히 맛있을 수 있단다. 한번 먹어보렴.
G: 알겠어요. 근데 다 먹고 나서 간식 먹어도 돼요? 치즈케이크나 마시멜로 같은 거요.

M: 딸은 다음에 무엇을 할 예정입니까?

(A) 채소까지 다 먹는다.
(B) 점심을 전부 다 먹는다.
(C) 보상으로 치즈케이크를 먹는다.

11.

M: Listen to a conversation between a mother and her daughter. Listen for the answer to this question.

G: Mom, why do you have so many lemons?

W: Kate, you're back from school early! I bought them to make lemonade and to clean the house.

G: You're going to use lemons to clean the house?

W: Yes, lemon juice is excellent for cleaning kitchen surfaces and even microwaves. All you need to do is rub it on the surfaces you want to clean. It kills germs and smells nice, too.

G: That's interesting! Is there anything I can do to help?

W: Thank you for offering. I've washed all the lemons, but I need to start cutting some into thin slices for the lemonade.

G: Great! Why don't you start cutting the lemons? I'll head over to the kitchen now.

M: What will the girl probably do next?

M: 엄마와 딸 사이의 대화를 듣고 질문에 답하세요.

G: 엄마, 레몬이 왜 이렇게 많아요?
W: Kate, 학교에서 일찍 왔구나. 레모네이드 만들고 집 청소에도 쓰려고 샀어.
G: 레몬으로 집을 청소할 건가요?
W: 응. 레몬주스는 주방은 물론 전자레인지까지 청소하는데 좋아. 청소하고 싶은 부분에 문지르기만 하면 된단다. 세균을 죽이고 냄새도 좋아.
G: 흥미롭네요! 제가 뭐 도와드릴 거 없을까요?
W: 도와주겠다니 고맙구나. 레몬은 다 씻었는데 레모네이드를 만드려면 얇게 자르기 시작해야 해.
G: 좋아요. 엄마는 레몬을 자르기 시작하면 어때요? 저는 지금 주방으로 갈게요.

M: 딸은 다음에 무엇을 할 예정입니까?

(A) 레몬을 슬라이스로 자른다.
(B) 레모네이드를 마신다.
(C) 주방을 청소한다.

12.

M: Listen to a conversation between two friends. Listen for the answer to this question.

B: It's my mom and dad's wedding anniversary soon, and I don't know what to get them.

G: How about pajamas? My parents loved them.

B: That sounds lovely, but I got them that last year. I was thinking of tickets to a musical, but they're really expensive.

G: Then how about flowers and cake?

B: Flowers sound great, but my parents don't like cake, so maybe I'll make them dinner.

M: What will the boy get for his parents' anniversary?

M: 두 친구 사이의 대화를 듣고 질문에 답하세요.

B: 곧 엄마 아빠 결혼기념일인데 뭘 사드려야 할지 모르겠어.

G: 잠옷 어때? 우리 부모님은 좋아하시던데.

B: 좋은데, 작년에 이미 사드렸어. 뮤지컬 티켓을 생각 중이었는데, 너무 비싸더라.

G: 그럼 꽃이랑 케이크는 어때?

B: 꽃 좋은 것 같아, 다만 부모님이 케이크를 좋아하지 않으셔서 저녁 식사를 만들어 드려야겠어.

M: 소년은 부모님 결혼기념일에 무엇을 해 드릴 것입니까?

(A) 잠옷
(B) 꽃
(C) 케이크

13.

M: Listen to a conversation between a mother and her son. Listen for the answer to this question.

B: Mom, can you drive me to the bookstore?

W: Right now? You woke up so early today. It's 8 a.m.! It's Saturday! You can sleep more.

B: The book I've been waiting months for is coming out today. I really want to buy it.

W: The bookstore doesn't even open until 10. Why do you want to leave so early? If we leave now, we will be there at 8:30. That's too early, and then you will have to wait outside for more than an hour and a half.

B: I know. But there'll be a long line of people all waiting to buy the book. I'm worried it will sell out. Can we please leave now?

M: What is the conversation about?

M: 엄마와 아들 사이의 대화를 듣고 질문에 답하세요.

B: 엄마, 저 서점에 데려다 주실 수 있어요?

W: 지금? 오늘 엄청 일찍 일어났네! 8시야. 토요일인데 좀 더 자도 되잖니.

B: 몇 달 동안 기다렸던 책이 오늘 나와요. 정말 사고 싶어요.

W: 근데 서점은 10시 되야 열잖아. 이렇게 일찍 가서 뭐 하려고? 지금 나가면 8시 30분쯤에 도착하니까 한 시간 반 넘게 밖에서 기다려야 해.

B: 알아요. 하지만 책을 사려는 사람들이 줄을 길게 설 거예요. 책이 다 팔릴까 걱정돼요. 지금 가면 안 될까요?

M: 이 대화는 무엇에 관한 이야기입니까?

(A) 아들이 일찍 가고 싶어 하는 이유
(B) 서점이 일찍 문을 여는 이유
(C) 책이 일찍 매진된 이유

14.

M: Listen to a conversation between a father and his son. Listen for the answer to this question.

M: What should we have for dinner?

B: Is mom working late today?

M: Yes, she is. She just called and said that she was running late.

B: Well, how about we order Chinese?

M: We've been ordering too much lately. How about we make dinner?

B: Sure, do you have anything in mind?

M: Maybe something with lots of vegetables?

B: Then salad with chicken? Or we could go with tacos.

M: No, I like your first suggestion. I had Mexican for lunch.

M: What will the boy and his dad have for dinner?

M: 아빠와 아들 사이의 대화를 듣고 질문에 답하세요.

M: 저녁으로 뭐 먹을까?

B: 오늘 엄마 늦게까지 일해요?

M: 응. 방금 전화 와서 늦는다고 하셨어.

B: 그럼 중국 음식 시킬까요?

M: 요즘 너무 자주 배달시켰잖아. 저녁 직접 만들어볼까?

B: 네. 생각하신 거 있어요?

M: 야채가 많이 들어간 음식 어때?

B: 그럼 치킨 샐러드요? 아니면 타코 먹을 수도 있고요.

M: 내가 점심에 멕시코 음식을 먹었으니까 첫 번째 걸로 먹자.

M: 아들과 아빠는 저녁으로 무엇을 먹을 예정입니까?

(A) 중국 음식
(B) 치킨 샐러드
(C) 타코

15.

M: Listen to a conversation between a boy and a girl. Listen for the answer to this question.

G: I think we have everything Mom asked us to buy.

B: Didn't she say plain milk? We got chocolate by mistake.

G: Nope, she said she needs chocolate milk to make milkshakes.

B: Oh, how about eggs? Didn't she say she needs a dozen? There are only six in this carton.

G: You're right, she did. Let's put it back and get a new one. Oh, and we forgot to get a loaf of bread.

B: Good point, but let's go to the egg section first.

M: What will the children do next?

M: 소년과 소녀 사이의 대화를 듣고 질문에 답하세요.

G: 엄마가 사 오라고 한 건 다 산 것 같아.

B: 엄마가 일반 우유 사라고 하지 않으셨어? 우린 실수로 초콜릿 우유 산 것 같은데.

G: 아니야. 엄마가 밀크셰이크 만든다고 초콜릿 우유 필요하다고 하셨어.

B: 아, 그럼 달걀은? 12개짜리 팩 하나 필요하다고 하지 않으셨어? 이 팩에는 6개밖에 없어.

G: 맞다. 이건 다시 가져다 두고 새 걸로 가져오자. 식빵 사는 것도 까먹었다.

B: 맞아. 그래도 달걀 코너 먼저 가자.

M: 아이들은 다음에 무엇을 할 예정입니까?

(A) 우유를 반품한다.
(B) 식빵을 산다.
(C) 달걀 팩을 바꾼다.

Part 3.

16.

W: Good morning, everyone! This is Principal Cindy. I know you are all very excited about our field trip to Disneyland on Friday. Please make sure to arrive at school by 7:30 a.m. Remember to bring a packed lunch and sunscreen and to wear comfortable shoes. All students are expected to behave well. I hope everyone has a great time on the field trip!

M: What did Principal Cindy ask the students?

W: 여러분, 좋은 아침이예요. Cindy 교장 선생님입니다. 이번 금요일에 있을 Disneyland 현장학습에 모두 신나 있으시죠. 학교에는 꼭 오전 7시 30분까지 도착하세요. 도시락, 자외선 차단제, 편한 신발 꼭 챙기고요. 모든 학생 여러분, 예의 있게 행동하길 바랍니다. 모두가 현장학습에서 즐거운 시간을 보내면 좋겠어요.

M: Cindy 교장 선생님이 학생들에게 요청한 것은 무엇입니까?

(A) 현장학습에 도시락을 가지고 오지 않기
(B) 금요일 오전 8시 30분에 학교 앞에서 만나기
(C) 현장학습에서 바르게 행동하기

17.

W: Hi Bella, it's Mom. I just got a phone call from your French teacher. She asked if you wanted to attend a French debate. It starts next month, and she thinks it'll be an excellent opportunity for you to meet other French students. I think so, too, and a chance like this doesn't come very often. How does it sound?

M: Why did Bella's mom call?

W: Bella, 엄마야. 방금 프랑스어 선생님께 전화가 왔어. 네가 프랑스어 토론회에 참가하고 싶은지 물어보셨어. 다음 달에 시작되는데, 다른 프랑스어 학습자를 만날 수 있는 좋은 기회라고 하시더라. 내 생각도 그래. 이런 기회는 자주 오는 게 아니잖니. 어때, 해볼래?

M: Bella의 엄마가 전화한 이유는 무엇입니까?

(A) Bella에게 곧 있을 토론회에 대한 생각을 묻기 위해
(B) Bella가 프랑스어를 배우고 싶은지 알아보기 위해
(C) Bella에게 프랑스어 선생님에게 전화하라고 말하기 위해

18.

W: Aaron, it's Sara. I know how much you wanted to attend the music festival this weekend, but there weren't any spots, right? Well, a spot just opened up! I have the tickets on hold, so call me back if you still want to go and don't have any other plans. Oh, I almost forgot that the tickets are for Sunday at 7 o'clock, not Saturday.

M: What will Aaron probably do?

W: Aaron, 나 Sara야. 이번 주말에 열리는 음악 축제에 매우 가고 싶어 했는데, 자리가 없었잖아. 방금 자리가 하나 났어! 내가 티켓을 보류해 놓았으니까, 아직 가고 싶은데 다른 계획이 없다면 나한테 꼭 연락해 줘. 아, 깜빡할 뻔했는데 티켓은 토요일이 아니라 일요일 7시 거야.

M: Aaron이 다음에 할 것은 무엇입니까?

(A) Sara에게 남은 자리에 대해 말해주기
(B) Sara에게 연락해서 음악 축제 참가 의사 알려주기
(C) 음악 축제 토요일 티켓에 대해 Sara에게 감사 인사하기

19.

W: Grace, it's Mom. I forgot to turn off the garage lights. Can you please turn them off when you get home? Also, the weather was excellent, so I could finally do the laundry. But I didn't have time to fold them, so I'd really appreciate it if you could neatly fold them and put them away. I've put 20 dollars on the kitchen table for you and your sister, so please make sure to order a healthy meal for your dinner.

M: What did Grace's mom NOT ask her to do?

W: Grace야, 엄마야. 차고 불 끄는 걸 깜빡했어. 집에 가면 꺼줄 수 있겠니? 그리고 오늘 날씨가 좋아서 빨래는 했는데. 시간이 없어서 개지를 못했어. 깔끔하게 개서 정리해 주면 고맙겠어. 너랑 동생 먹으라고 부엌 식탁 위에 20달러 놔뒀어. 건강한 저녁 시켜 먹도록 해.

M: Grace의 엄마가 부탁하지 <u>않은</u> 것은 무엇입니까?

(A) 세탁기 돌리기
(B) 옷 정리하고 개기
(C) 영양가 있는 저녁 식사하기

20.

W: Hello, Mrs. Woods. This is Principal Robinson. Thank you for being the head of the parent council again this year. I wanted to discuss parent volunteer opportunities at our school. While many parents have signed up to help with lunch, we do not have many volunteers for the drop-off zone or as crossing guards. Do you think the early-morning timing might be a reason? I know mornings can be busy for everyone, but I'd love to find some solutions. Could we meet for a cup of coffee to discuss this before the parent meeting this afternoon?

M: Why did the principal call?

W: 여보세요, Woods 학부모님. Robinson 교장입니다. 올해도 학부모 회장으로 수고해 주셔서 감사합니다. 학부모 자원봉사 기회에 대해 말씀드리고자 전화 드렸습니다. 점심시간 도우미에는 많은 학부모님들이 신청해 주셨지만, 등교 시간 하차 구역이나 횡단보도 안내 도우미를 신청해 주신 분은 많지 않습니다. 아침 시간대라서 그런 것일까요? 모두 바쁜 시간이라는 것을 알지만, 해결책을 함께 찾아보고 싶습니다. 오늘 오후에 있을 학부모 회의 전에 잠시 만나서 커피 한잔하며 이야기 나눌 수 있을까요?

M: 교장 선생님이 전화를 건 이유는 무엇입니까?

(A) 자신이 자원봉사자로서 할 수 있는 일의 종류에 대해 묻기 위해
(B) 문제 논의를 위해 Woods 학부모님이 만날 수 있는지 확인하기 위해
(C) 올해 새롭게 생긴 자원봉사 기회에 대해 논의하는 데 관심이 있어서

21.

M: Hey Olivia, it's your granddad. I hope you had a great day at school! Your mom told me that you haven't been getting a good night's sleep. Are the upcoming tests causing you a lot of stress? While studying is very important, remember that eating well and getting enough sleep is even more important. As you know, I run every morning, and it really helps me stay alert during the day. I'm usually exhausted by the time I hit the bed. How about you give it a try? I can pick you up every morning at eight!

M: Why did Olivia's grandad call?

M: 안녕 Olivia, 할아버지란다. 학교에서 좋은 하루 보냈니? 엄마에게 네가 요즘 잠을 잘 못 자고 있다고 들었어. 다가오는 시험 때문에 스트레스를 많이 받고 있니? 공부도 물론 중요하지만, 잘 먹고 충분히 자는 게 훨씬 더 중요하단다. 알다시피 나는 매일 아침 달리기를 해. 그게 하루 종일 정신을 맑게 유지하는 데 큰 도움이 된단다. 잠자리에 들 때쯤이면 피곤해서 숙면을 취할 수 있고. 한번 해보는게 어때? 매일 아침 8시에 데리러 갈 수 있단다.

M: Olivia의 할아버지가 전화한 이유는 무엇입니까?

(A) Olivia와 조깅을 하기를 원해서
(B) Olivia가 매일 아침 달리기를 하고 있는지 물으려고
(C) Olivia가 시험 준비에 도움이 필요한지 궁금해서

22.

B: Hey Jin, it's your brother Brian. Dad just texted me to say that neither he nor Mom can pick us up from school today. Since I have soccer practice every Tuesday and Thursday, I can't walk you home. The finals are this Friday, and I can't miss practice, so I'm sorry about that. If you can't walk home by yourself, could you call Aunt Natalie to pick you up? I've already talked to her, so she's expecting your call. Don't forget to give her a ring during lunch. Have a great day!

M: What will Jin's aunt do next?

B: Jin, 나 Brian 형이야. 아빠가 방금 문자를 보내셨는데, 오늘 엄마랑 아빠 둘 다 학교에 우리를 데리러 올 수 없대. 나는 매주 화요일과 목요일에 축구 연습이 있어서 너랑 같이 집까지 걸어갈 수 없어. 이번 주 금요일이 결승전이라 연습을 빠질 수가 없거든, 미안해. 네가 혼자 집에 못 가면, Natalie 이모에게 전화해서 데리러 와달라고 할래? 내가 이미 말씀드려서 네 전화를 기다리고 계실 거야. 점심시간에 꼭 전화해. 좋은 하루 보내!

M: Jin의 이모가 다음에 할 것은 무엇입니까?

(A) Jin의 학교로 향한다.
(B) Jin의 전화를 기다린다.
(C) 학교 앞에서 기다린다.

23.

G: Hi, Dad, it's Meredith. I'm trying to make a presentation on my laptop, but I need some help. I don't know how to insert the pictures into the slides. I've already downloaded all the images and noted where I want to place them. Could you help me? The presentation isn't due until next week, so we have some time. Using the computer is still a little tricky for me.

M: Why did Meredith call her dad?

G: 아빠, Meredith예요. 노트북으로 발표 자료를 만들고 있는데 도움이 필요해요. 사진을 슬라이드에 어떻게 넣어야 할지 모르겠어요. 이미지는 다 다운로드했고 어디에 배치할지도 다 적어 놨어요. 도와주실 수 있어요? 발표는 다음 주까지라서 시간은 좀 있어요. 컴퓨터 쓰는 게 아직 저한테는 좀 어려워요.

M: Meredith가 아빠에게 전화한 이유는 무엇입니까?

(A) 발표 대본을 기억하는 데 도움이 필요해서
(B) 원하는 사진을 다운로드하는 방법을 몰라서
(C) 발표 슬라이드에 사진 올리는 방법을 몰라서

24.

B: Vince, it's Alex. Miss Jackson told me that your sports bag was in the lost-and-found. She told me to tell you that you need to pick it up today, as you have swim practice tomorrow. She said something about needing your swim fins for practice, so I suggest you come and pick it up. Since it's Friday, the lost-and-found office just closed, so make sure to stop by the main office before five o'clock. It's already three o'clock so you only have two hours left.

M: What will Vince do next?

B: Vince, Alex야. Jackson 선생님이 네 스포츠 가방이 분실물 보관소에 있다고 말씀하셨어. 내일 수영 연습이 있으니 오늘 찾아가야 한다고 전해달라고 하셨어. 연습에 수영 오리발이 필요하다고 말씀하셨으니까, 와서 찾아가는 게 좋을 거야. 금요일이라서 분실물 보관소는 방금 문을 닫았으니까, 다섯 시 전에 본관 사무실에 들러야 해. 벌써 3시니까 2시간 밖에 남지 않았어.

M: Vince가 다음에 할 행동이 무엇입니까?

(A) 분실물 보관소에 가기
(B) 수영 연습하러 가기
(C) 본관 사무실 가기

25.

G: Mrs. Gibson, hi, it's Chloe. I just got the call that I got the leading role in the musical! Your drama classes have been very helpful, and I couldn't have done it without your support. The practice starts next week, and the show is in three months. I am so excited to meet the other performers and am looking forward to getting in sync!

M: Why did Chloe call Mrs. Gibson?

G: Gibson 선생님, 안녕하세요, Chloe예요. 방금 뮤지컬 주연을 맡게 되었다는 연락을 받았어요. 선생님의 연극 수업이 정말 도움이 되었고, 선생님의 지원 없이는 해낼 수 없을 거예요. 연습은 다음 주에 시작하고, 공연은 세 달 뒤예요. 다른 출연진들을 만날 생각에 너무 신나고, 호흡을 맞춰나가는 것이 기대돼요.

M: Chloe가 Gibson 선생님에게 전화한 이유는 무엇입니까?

(A) 공연이 곧 시작된다는 기쁜 소식을 알리기 위해
(B) Gibson 선생님의 격려에 감사의 뜻을 전하기 위해
(C) 뮤지컬을 보러 가는 것이 얼마나 기대되는지 말하기 위해

Part 4.

[26-29] 다음을 듣고, 26-29번 질문에 답하세요.

W: "Wow, you actually saw a UFO? An actual UFO? Are you sure you're not mistaking it for a plane or a drone?" David asked in disbelief. "I'm positive! I saw it with my sister, Lily. She was the one who pointed up at the sky and told me to look at it. It flew by so fast that we couldn't take a picture; it all happened in a matter of seconds," Diane replied excitedly.
The two children were sitting outside, enjoying ice cream while gazing at the summer night sky. They both loved exploring space. Whenever they were together, they looked up and wondered what was out there.
"Well, lucky you! I've never seen one before, but I would love to. Diane, do you think aliens exist? There are videos and pictures that people claim to have seen them, but I've never seen one with my own eyes, so I don't believe they're real," David said.
Diane rolled her eyes; this wasn't the first time David had insisted that Earth was the only planet with life forms. "Think about it, David. The universe is enormous. It's the largest expanse we know of. What makes you think there isn't other life out there? The Earth isn't even the biggest planet, and there are so many things in space that scientists don't even know about yet," Diane pointed out.
David knew what Diane was going to say. Even though he didn't believe in aliens, he loved to joke about the topic. "It's true, but extraterrestrials in space? That sounds a bit silly to me. I'll only believe it when I see one with my own eyes!" he laughed.

W: "와, 너 진짜 UFO 봤다고? 진짜 UFO? 비행기나 드론이랑 착각한 거 아니지?" David가 믿을 수 없다는 듯 물었습니다. "확실해! Lily 언니랑 같이 봤어. 언니가 하늘을 가리키면서 보라고 했거든. 너무 빨리 날아가서 사진도 못 찍었어. 눈 깜짝할 사이에 벌어진 일이야." Diane이 신나서 대답했습니다.
두 아이는 밖에 앉아 아이스크림을 즐기며 여름 밤 하늘을 바라보고 있었습니다. 둘 다 우주 탐험을 무척 좋아해서, 함께 있을 때마다 하늘을 올려다보며 저 밖에 무엇이 있을지 궁금해했습니다.
"음, 운 좋네! 난 한 번도 본 적 없지만, 꼭 보고 싶다. Diane, 너는 외계인이 존재한다고 생각해? 사람들이 봤다고 주장하는 동영상이나 사진들은 있지만, 난 내 눈으로 직접 본 적이 없어서 진짜라고 믿지 않아." David가 말했습니다.

Diane이 눈을 굴렸습니다. David가 지구가 생명체가 있는 유일한 행성이라고 고집한 것이 처음은 아니었습니다. "생각해 봐, David. 우주는 거대해. 우리가 아는 가장 넓은 공간이야. 왜 저 밖에 다른 생명체가 없다고 생각해? 지구는 가장 큰 행성도 아니고, 우주에는 과학자들도 아직 모르는 것들이 너무 많아." Diane이 짚어 주었습니다. David는 Diane이 무슨 말을 할지 알고 있었습니다. 비록 외계인의 존재를 믿지 않았지만, 그는 이 주제로 농담하는 것을 좋아했습니다. "그건 맞지만, 우주에 외계인이 있다고? 나한테는 좀 우스꽝스럽게 들려. 내 눈으로 직접 봐야 믿을 거야!" 그가 웃으며 말했습니다.

26. Diane이 UFO 사진을 못 찍은 이유는 무엇입니까?

(A) 명확하게 보지 못해서
(B) 눈 깜짝할 사이에 지나가서
(C) Lily 언니가 빨리 말해주지 않아서

27. Diane과 David는 함께 대부분의 시간을 어떻게 보냅니까?

(A) 아이스크림을 먹으며
(B) 외계인에 대해 논쟁하며
(C) 하늘을 바라보고 지구 너머에 무엇이 존재하는지 생각하며

해설 David과 Diane은 함께 있는 동안 하늘을 바라보며 우주 저편에 무엇이 있는지 궁금해하는 모습이 묘사되어 있으므로, 선택지 (C)가 정답이다.

28. David가 외계인의 존재를 믿지 않는 이유는 무엇입니까?

(A) UFO는 봤지만 외계인은 보지 못해서
(B) 직접 본 적이 없어서
(C) Diane이 항상 농담한다고 생각해서

해설 David이 외계인이 있다는 것을 믿지 않는 이유는, 사람들이 비디오나 사진을 통해 봤다고 주장하지만 자신은 직접 본 적이 없기 때문이라고 나와 있으므로, 보기 (B)가 정답이다.

29. Diane이 눈을 굴린 이유는 무엇입니까?

(A) David와 이 대화를 이전에 해본 적이 있어서
(B) 자신이 UFO를 봤다고 너무 여러 번 설명했기 때문에
(C) David가 과학적 사실을 왜 믿지 않는지 이해할 수 없기 때문에

[30-33] 다음을 듣고, 30-33번 질문에 답하세요.

> M: Did you know that a century ago, there were hardly any female pilots? Today, we celebrate amazing women in aviation, thanks in part to pioneers such as Amelia Earhart! Known for her adventurous spirit, Amelia inspired people worldwide with her determination.
> From a young age, her mom encouraged her to be bold. While most girls played with dolls, Amelia climbed trees and was often described as a tomboy. At the age of ten, she saw her first airplane, but she wasn't impressed, as

it didn't seem interesting to her. But everything changed when she took a ride at an airfield with her dad at 23, and that is when she discovered her passion for flying! Amelia became the first woman to fly solo across the Atlantic and she is famous for completing many record-breaking flights. However, her journey began in 1928 when she crossed the Atlantic as part of a crew. In 1932, she flew solo for the first time!
> Tragically, in 1937, although she wanted to fly around the globe, during her final flight over the Pacific with navigator Fred Noonan, their plane vanished without a trace.
> Although her disappearance remains a mystery, Amelia is still an inspiring figure for many today!

M: 백 년 전만 해도 여성 조종사가 거의 없었다는 것을 알고 계셨습니까? 오늘날 우리가 항공 분야의 뛰어난 여성들을 기념할 수 있게 된 것은 Amelia Earhart와 같은 선구자들 덕분입니다. 모험 정신으로 유명한 Amelia는 그녀의 투지로 전 세계 사람들에게 영감을 주었습니다.
어린 시절부터 그녀의 어머니는 그녀에게 대담해지라고 격려했습니다. 대부분의 여자아이들이 인형을 가지고 놀 때, Amelia는 나무를 오르며 말괄량이 소녀로 불리곤 했습니다. 열 살 때 처음으로 비행기를 보았지만 당시에는 별로 흥미를 못 느꼈습니다. 하지만 23살에 아버지와 함께 비행장에서 비행을 하면서 모든 것이 바뀌었고, 그때 그녀는 비행에 대한 열정을 발견하게 되었습니다!
Amelia는 대서양을 단독으로 횡단한 최초의 여성이 되었으며, 수많은 기록인 비행을 성공적으로 마친 것으로 유명합니다. 하지만 그녀의 여정은 1928년 승무원의 일원으로 대서양을 횡단한 것에서 시작되었습니다. 이후 1932년에 처음으로 단독 비행에 성공했습니다. 비극적이게도, 1937년 그녀는 세계 일주 비행을 원했지만, 항해사 Fred Noonan과 함께 태평양 상공을 비행하던 중 그들의 비행기는 흔적도 없이 사라졌습니다. 그녀의 실종은 여전히 미스터리로 남아 있지만, Amelia는 오늘날에도 많은 사람들에게 영감을 주는 인물로 남아있습니다!

30. Amelia가 유명한 조종사인 이유는 무엇입니까?

(A) 조종사로서 많은 기록을 깼다.
(B) 당시 최초의 여성 조종사였다.
(C) 세계 일주 비행으로 유명하다.

해설 Amelia는 세계를 비행하고 싶었지만 1937년 태평양을 지날 때 비행기가 사라졌고, 여성 최초의 파일럿은 아니라고 언급되어 있어 선택지 (B)와 (C)는 사실과 다르며, 여러 기록적인 비행을 한 점에서 그녀가 유명한 파일럿이라는 내용이 제시되었으므로 정답은 (A)이다.

31. 그녀에게 조종사가 되도록 영감을 준 것은 무엇입니까?

(A) 아버지가 조종사여서 그녀를 격려했다.
(B) 비행기에 대한 그녀의 사랑은 첫눈에 반한 것이었다.
(C) 처음으로 비행기를 탔던 경험을 운명으로 느꼈다.

32. Amelia에 대해 사실인 것은 무엇입니까?

(A) 1932년 태평양 상공에서 마지막 비행을 했다.
(B) 1932년 대서양을 단독으로 처음 비행했다.
(C) 1932년 승무원의 일원으로 대서양을 횡단한 최초의 여성이었다.

해설 Amelia Earhart는 1928년 대서양 횡단 비행에 승무원으로 참여했지만 직접 조종하지는 않았고, 1932년에는 여성 최초로 대서양을 단독 비행했으며, 1937년 지구 일주를 시도하던 중 실종되어 이는 그녀의 마지막 비행으로 언급되었기 때문에 정답은 (B)이다.

33. 본문에서 Amelia에 대해 언급되지 <u>않은</u> 내용은 무엇입니까?

(A) 많은 사람이 다양한 이유로 그녀를 존경한다.
(B) 마지막 비행에서 무선 연결이 끊겼다.
(C) Fred Noonan은 그녀의 항해사이자 남편이었다.

[34-36] 다음을 듣고, 34-36번 질문에 답하세요.

M: Bread is one of the most loved foods worldwide. Its many shapes and sizes make it a delightful treat packed with all sorts of flavors. You can enjoy bread for breakfast, lunch, dinner, or even dessert. However, in the past, bread was not a common food; only wealthy people could afford it. Nonetheless, did you know that bread is good for more than just eating? It has a fun history that goes back over 10,000 years, and people have found many interesting ways to use it.

Artists and writers didn't have rubber erasers back then like we do now. Instead, they would use a piece of white bread to fix their pencil or charcoal mistakes! Also, during the Middle Ages, when real plates were not so easy to get, people came up with the idea to use thick, stale bread as their dining plates! They would pile their food on it and could even snack on the leftover bread afterward.

These days, bread can still surprise us with its creative uses. If you find a slice of stale white bread lying around, don't throw it away! Put it to work and use it as a cleaning sponge! It's great for dusting off paintings and wallpaper. Also, no special cleaners are needed, so bread makes it an eco-friendly option too! So, think outside the box next time you have some stale bread, and give it a new life!

M: 빵은 전 세계에서 가장 사랑받는 음식 중 하나입니다. 다양한 모양과 크기는 온갖 맛이 가득한 즐거운 음식을 선사합니다. 빵은 아침, 점심, 저녁 식사 또는 심지어 디저트로도 즐길 수 있습니다. 하지만 과거에는 빵이 흔한 음식이 아니었으며, 부유한 사람들만이 살 수 있었습니다. 그럼에도 불구하고, 빵이 단순히 먹는 것 외에도 유용하다는 사실을 알고 계셨나요? 빵은 10,000년 이상 거슬러 올라가는 흥미로운 역사를 가지고 있으며, 사람들은 빵을 다양한 방법으로 활용해 왔습니다.

과거에는 화가와 작가들에게 지금과 같은 고무 지우개가 없었습니다. 대신, 그들은 연필로 쓴 것이나 목탄으로 잘못 그린 것을 고칠 때 흰 빵 조각을 사용했습니다. 또한, 중세 시대에는 접시를 구하기 쉽지 않아 두껍고 딱딱한 빵을 접시로 사용하는 것을 생각해 냈습니다. 그 위에 음식을 올렸고, 식사가 끝나면 남은 빵을 간식으로 먹기도 했습니다.

요즘에도 빵은 창의적인 용도로 우리를 놀라게 할 수 있습니다. 오래된 흰 빵 조각이 여기저기 놓여 있다면, 버리지 마세요. 그것을 청소용 스펀지로 사용해 보세요. 그림이나 벽지의 먼지를 털어내는 데 아주 좋습니다. 특별한 세제도 필요 없으므로 빵은 친환경적인 선택이기도 합니다. 그러니 다음에 오래된 빵이 있다면 고정관념을 깨고 새로운 용도를 찾아보세요!

34. 과거 화가들이 흰 빵을 사용한 이유는 무엇입니까?

(A) 실수를 고치기 위해
(B) 붓과 함께 사용하는 흔한 재료여서
(C) 무언가를 지울 때 저렴한 선택지여서

35. 집을 청소할 때 주로 어떤 빵을 사용합니까?

(A) 신선한 흰 빵
(B) 따뜻한 갈색 빵
(C) 굳어버린 흰 빵

36. 빵을 사용할 수 있는 방법으로 언급되지 <u>않은</u> 것은 무엇입니까?

(A) 접시 대신 사용할 수 있다.
(B) 화가들이 그림을 그리는 데 사용했다.
(C) 먼지를 닦는 데 사용할 수 있다.

[37-39] 다음을 듣고, 37-39번 질문에 답하세요.

W: The beautiful flowers we see outside are colorful and often have a pleasant fragrance. However, they don't just look pretty; they play a crucial role in attracting insects such as butterflies and bees. These insects help in the process of pollination, which is essential for the production of fruit and the growth of new flowers and plants.

Plants consist of various parts, each with a special role. Let's start with the roots. As you might have guessed, roots are located underground, and their primary role is to absorb nutrients and water from the soil. This essential nourishment travels up the stem. The stem acts like a straw, transporting these minerals to the rest of the plant. It also serves as a strong anchor, supporting and preventing the flower from toppling over. Next, we have the leaves. They function much like chefs, using sunlight, water, and gas from the air called carbon dioxide to create food for the plant. This process produces glucose, which is a type of sugar that serves as nourishment for the plant. Additionally, leaves release oxygen, which is vital for our survival. This remarkable process is known as photosynthesis.

W: 우리가 밖에서 보는 아름다운 꽃들은 다채로운 색을 띠고 있으며 향기로운 냄새를 풍깁니다. 하지만 꽃은 단지 보기 좋은 것에 그치는 것이 아니라, 나비나 벌과 같은 곤충들을 유인하는 데 중요한 역할을 합니다. 이 곤충들은 수분 과정에 도움을 주는데, 이는 열매를 맺고 새로운 꽃과 식물이 자라는 데 필수적입니다.

식물은 다양한 부분으로 구성되어 있는데, 각 부분은 특별한 역할을 합니다. 먼저 뿌리부터 살펴보겠습니다. 예상하셨겠지만, 뿌리는 땅 속에 위치하며, 주된 역할은 토양에서 영양분과 물을 흡수하는 것입니다. 이렇게 흡수된 필수 영양분은 줄기를 타고 위로 이동합니다. 줄기는 빨대처럼 작용하여 이러한 무기물을 식물의 다른 부분으로 운반합니다. 줄기는 강력한 닻처럼 꽃을 지지하여 쓰러지지 않도록 합니다. 다음은 잎입니다. 잎은 요리사처럼, 햇빛, 물, 공기 중의 이산화탄소를 사용하여 식물이 먹을 음식을 만듭니다. 이 과정은 식물의 영양분으로 작용하는 일종의 설탕인 포도당을 생산합니다. 또한, 잎은 우리의 생존에 필수적인 산소를 방출합니다. 이 놀라운 과정을 광합성이라고 합니다.

37. 수분은 무엇입니까?

(A) 수분은 꽃이 화려한 색을 유지하도록 돕는다.
(B) 수분은 이산화탄소를 만드는 방법이다.
(C) 수분은 꽃이 새로운 식물을 만들 수 있도록 돕는다.

해설 꽃은 알록달록한 색깔과 향기 뿐만 아니라 곤충을 끌어들이는 중요한 역할을 하며, 이로 인해 수분이 이루어지고 새로운 식물이 자랄 수 있다고 지문에 제시되어 있으므로, 정답은 (C)이다.

38. 줄기의 역할이 <u>아닌</u> 것은 무엇입니까?

(A) 꽃이 쓰러지지 않도록 지탱한다.
(B) 꽃에 영양분을 전달한다.
(C) 당분을 만들어낸다.

해설 줄기는 꽃이 넘어지지 않도록 지지해 주고, 다른 꽃들에게 필요한 영양분을 전달하는 역할을 한다고 나와 있으며, 포도당을 생산하는 것은 줄기가 아니라 잎이기 때문에 정답은 (C)이다.

39. 잎은 어떤 일을 합니까?

(A) 햇빛을 이용해 먹을 것을 만든다.
(B) 땅 속으로 부터 영양분을 흡수한다.
(C) 꽃을 지탱해 주는 역할을 한다.

해설 잎은 햇빛, 물, 이산화탄소를 이용해 식물에 필요한 영양분을 만드는 광합성을 수행하며, 이 과정에서 사람에게 필요한 산소도 공급한다. 또한, 토양에 있는 영양분을 흡수하는 것은 잎이 아니라 뿌리이며, 꽃이 넘어지지 않도록 지지하는 역할은 줄기가 한다. 따라서 정답은 (A)이다.

Ace the
TOEFL Primary
Step 2